CREATION

CREATION

IN THE BEGINNING GOD CREATED THE HEAVEN AND THE EARTH
GENESIS 1:1

JOHN METCALFE

THE PUBLISHING TRUST
CHURCH ROAD, TYLERS GREEN, PENN, BUCKINGHAMSHIRE.

Printed and Published by
John Metcalfe Publishing Trust
Church Road, Tylers Green
Penn, Buckinghamshire

—

Distributed by Trust Representatives
and Agents world-wide

In the Far East

Bethany, Orchard Point P.O. Box 0373
Singapore 912313

—

—

First Published November 1996

—

ISBN 1 870039 71 8

—

CONTENTS

CREATION

I

The Testimony to Creation

IN the beginning God created the heaven and the earth, Genesis 1:1. Or as Exodus 20:11 elaborates, 'In six days the LORD made heaven and earth, the sea, and all that in them is, and rested the seventh day: wherefore the LORD blessed the sabbath day, and hallowed it.'

But who believes that literally in these days? Well, I will tell you who believed it literally in days gone by.

For example, the most upright and holy men the world has ever known, throughout all generations, whose rectitude, resolution, endurance, intelligence, feeling, intuition, compassion, and whole interior spiritual development leaves the fig leaves of the modern academic or pseudo-scientific 'rationalist' in pathetic tatters.

Take John, for instance, of whom the Holy Ghost testifies, 'He that saw it bare record, and his record is true: and he knoweth that he saith true, that ye might believe', Jn. 19:35.

But whatever has the Holy Ghost testified of those people whose speculations attempt to overturn the truth of Creation, whose eyes gloss over but a surface, who mind earthly things, and see nothing invisible?

What, I say, in comparison with the sight of John whose vision reached from one end of heaven to the other, whose insight penetrated the heights and depths of the deity, and whose inspired gaze spanned the ages in their entirety from the beginning of the world until the end of it, till time shall be no more.

Listen: 'In the beginning was the Word, and the Word was with God, and the Word was God. The same was in the beginning with God. All things were made by him; and without him was not any thing made that was made', Jn. 1:1-3.

And again, writing of that Word by whom all things were created, who was with God, and was God, John states, 'He was in the world, and the world was made by him, and the world knew him not', John 1:10. Once more, 'I saw a new heaven and a new earth: for the first heaven and the first earth were passed away; and there was no more sea', Rev. 21:1.

John believed that in the beginning God created the heaven and the earth, and he believed it literally.

Now consider Peter, the very chiefest of the apostles, of whose strict rectitude and humble self-discipline—hence, therefore, applied caution in relation to the facts—there can be less doubt than anyone the world has ever known. Yet he believed literally that 'In the beginning God created the heaven and the earth'.

Peter refers prophetically to the uniformitarian prejudice of latter-day scientists; only he does not call them scientists, he calls them scoffers. 'There shall come in the last days scoffers, walking after their own lusts, and saying, Where is the promise of his coming? for since the fathers fell asleep, all things continue as they were from the beginning of the creation', II Pet. 3:3,4.

In this place Peter shows that he believed in the Creation from the beginning; whereas scoffers contend for uniformitarianism without a beginning.

More. Peter believed in the Creation in six days, for, inspired of God, he points not only to Creation itself but also specifically to the second day of its existence—Genesis 1:6-8—declaring 'By the word of God the heavens were of old', adding 'the earth standing out of the water and in the water.'

This state, resulting from the forming of the firmament, was the means of the flood: 'Whereby the world that then was, being overflowed with water, perished', II Pet. 3:3-6.

Jude is yet another apostolic authority. He had no doubt of the exactitude of his chronology when, inspired of God, by the Holy Ghost he wrote, 'Enoch also, the seventh from Adam'.

And if Jude could count the genealogies from the first man with such precision, who was divinely inspired to write the infallible scripture, the fact of Adam's creation in the day in which he was created, besides the truth that 'In the beginning God created the heaven and the earth', cannot be doubted.

This is that holy man's testimony to all generations of the dependable nature of the first chapters of Genesis.

Nor should the divine testimony of this apostolic author once be doubted. But we all know that those bigoted scientists—

3

so-called—who wish to overturn the truth of Creation would object that however holy, Jude was neither a scientist, nor was he in possession of current scientific data.

That is true. But the scientists who are in possession of that data draw such hypothetical conclusions from it, that they no longer deserve the name of scientist.

Whereas without professing the name of scientist, nor possessing that sum of scientific data, free from the ungodliness which detests the Creator, and void of that bigotry which prefers vain hypotheses to the truth of Creation, Jude, by sticking to the realities and facts revealed, deserves the name of scientist more than they do, and his epistle the title of data more than their pathetic little heap of facts does.

And will they say of Jude what they say of the Creator? Will they extend their contempt by declaring, Who was he, and where is his work, that we may tell it? To them, neither has an existence worth their attention.

What then will they say of the great king David, whose supernatural insight, prophetic vision, and divine attestation they cannot deny? Nor can they deny his unerring spiritual inspiration, a thing of which they themselves are void.

But the holy king, in the power of the Spirit of God, gave forth this immutable witness, Psalm 119:160, 'Thy word is true from the beginning'. The beginning, mark: not after the first few chapters are dismissed.

True from the first verse of the first chapter. This states 'In the beginning God created the heaven and the earth.'

Again the great king, who dwelt in God's holy temple, and beheld the glory of the LORD—things quite absent from these speculators over scraps of information—I say, David declared,

Psalm 102:25, 'Of old hast thou laid the foundation of the earth', and again, Psalm 104:5, he affirms that God by his own power formed the world in the beginning.

And what shall we say of the apostle Paul? After all, however men pretend to objective detachment as to scientific facts, the character of a man precedes his work, and his subjective condition anticipates his objectivity, no matter what his profession.

But what man among them will dare to compare himself in character with Paul? Or what subjective love among them brought forth works remotely bearing the least comparison with the awesome and immortal objective good wrought by Paul, who, being dead, yet speaketh?

Besides all this, to what scientist did Christ ever appear in glory on some Damascus road? What divine call from heaven have they—from the least to the greatest—ever received? What ministry was once entrusted to them from the heaven of heavens by the Most High? or when did Father, Son, and Holy Ghost ever infallibly guide their writings, or grant to them the working of such divine and supernatural miracles? By so much is their word comparable to Paul's.

Paul tells us, Romans 5:14, 'Death reigned from Adam to Moses'. Then, if Moses was a real person, so was Adam. With this difference: one was begotten, the other created.

And so Paul teaches, using the very words of Genesis: 'The first man Adam was made'—mark that, *made*—'a living soul.' And again 'Adam was first *formed*', I Tim. 2:13. It follows, Adam had a Maker, namely, he from whom his form was derived. Whence it is evident, Adam was the first man, he was literally a man, and he was divinely and immediately created to be man.

Or do these think to know better than Almighty God, the Lord Jesus Christ, the Spirit of God, and the holy apostles and prophets? If so, such men demonstrate to a scientific nicety that, spiritually, 'In Adam all die', I Cor. 15:22.

Or will the heights of the speculative impiety of such scientists —improperly taking scientifically established facts as the basis of their conjectural hypotheses—dare to challenge the Son of God, 'In whom are hid all the treasures of wisdom and knowledge', Col. 2:3?

Then if, I Cor. 1:30, Of God Christ Jesus is made unto us wisdom, it is clear that the imparting of this heavenly wisdom is a divine favour which has clean escaped evolutionary and uniformitarian scientists.

For had God made Christ Jesus to be their wisdom, they would have attended to his speech: 'Thou, Lord, in the beginning hast laid the foundation of the earth; and the heavens are the works of thine hands', Hebrews 1:10.

But this truth these people clearly cannot abide, and, like Satan, would attempt to overturn the work of the Creator. Then who is their master, wittingly or unwittingly? Such, given to folly, ought from their nativity to have hearkened to the wise man, 'Remember now thy Creator in the days of thy youth'. This late, it may well prove too late.

They should at least give objective and scientific consideration to the question, since they cannot render subjective and suited humility, 'Where wast thou when I laid the foundations of the earth?', Job 38:4.

Well, where were they? Not remotely in existence. Then will they attempt to overturn the works and observations of one who *was* there, who was in the beginning with God, and was God, without whom was nothing made that was made? Yes they will, and by this, all men should mark their ungodly, not to say ludicrous, conceit.

And what did he work and observe, who was in the beginning? He wrought what he observed, and he noted the fruitfulness of his work. And so it is written, 'And God saw that it was good', Genesis 1:4,10,12,18,21,25.

Indeed, after the creation of man it was said, 'And God saw that it was very good', Gen. 1:31. But what good can God possibly see in these so-called scientists of aeons later, who see nothing but bad, and attempt no less than to argue the Creator out of his Creation, and the Creation out of its existence?

Then where were they? What did they see? Nothing. Absolutely nothing. It is written, 'And God saw the light, that it was good', Genesis 1:4. But these who were not there presume it to be different: they see the darkness, and it is bad. And if the light that is in them be darkness, how great is that darkness? Mt. 6:23.

However, take notice of the truth that, Gen. 1:4,5, God divided the light from the darkness. And God called the light Day, and the darkness he called Night. And since to this very hour 'Day unto day uttereth speech, and night unto night showeth knowledge', Psalm 19:2, what notice ought we to take of fools who neither hear the speech of day, nor receive the knowledge of night, but contradict both?

They contradict the Son of God to his teeth. What! These latter-day conceited specks? I say, Where were they when he laid the foundations of the earth, in the day that the sons of God shouted for joy, Job 38:7?

And will these, whose breath is in their nostrils, whose life is but a span, whose speculation is borrowed, whose element is darkness, I say, will these contradict the true God, and eternal life, whose goings have been from everlasting, whose name shall be called Jesus, for he shall save his people from their sins? But, evidently, not save these people from their sins, else they had not trodden underfoot the Son of God.

7

But pause: hearken to the voice of the Son; pay attention to his speech, who was both at the Creation, was the Creator, and saw what he had created.

'Had ye believed Moses'—who wrote Genesis in the beginning—'Ye would have believed me', Jn. 5:46,47. Evolutionary and uniformitarian 'scientists'—falsely so called—by profession do not believe Moses. Then, they cannot believe Christ.

But he said 'Thy word is truth', John 17:17. Not, *some* of thy word is truth: *all* of it is truth. For, Psalm 119:160, Thy word is true from the beginning, and, if so, from Genesis 1:1. 'And the scripture cannot be broken', John 10:35.

However, all who fall on this Stone shall be broken, yea, and ground to powder. Then he that sitteth in the heavens shall laugh: the Lord shall have them in derision.

Contradict the Son of God? As well might they command the winds not to blow; the tides not to rise; the earth not to bring forth and bud; the day not to dawn or the night not to fall. As well order the sun to cease from rising; the moon to refrain from setting; the stars to forbear from shining; or the planets to stop from orbiting.

As well demand sound to be silence, and silence to be sound; cold to be heat, and heat to be cold. As well to charge the rivers to turn back, or the seas to empty; the darkness to be called day, or the light to be called night.

Who are these? They are nothing but the same as those inexcusable persons described in Rom. 1:20, 'For the invisible things of him from the creation of the world are clearly seen, being understood by the things that are made, even his eternal power and Godhead; so that they are without excuse.' Professing themselves to be wise, they have become fools, Romans 1:22.

The Son of God, called the wisdom of God, named the truth, dwelling in light unapproachable, who cannot deny himself, who created all things, speaks of the things which he created and made, declaring out of the fulness of his everlasting deity. Now listen. 'But from the beginning of the creation God made them male and female', Mark 10:6.

Whence observe that there was a Creation, not an evolution. That this Creation had a beginning, not a uniformitarian procession. And that God made them male and female by his own immediate divine and creative power, they did not become what they were because of any species existent before their creation.

Now this is the word that shall stand. The word of liars shall not stand. Their words shall fall. The word of the Lord endureth for ever. Their word shall perish. And in that day the folly of such shall be made manifest unto all men.

In what day? In the day when God shall judge the secrets of men by Jesus Christ according to my gospel, Romans 2:16. Because he hath appointed a day in the which he will judge the world in righteousness by that man whom he hath ordained; whereof he hath given assurance unto all men, in that he hath raised him from the dead, Acts 17:31.

And, say the apostles, who ate and drank with him after he rose from the dead, 'He commanded us to preach unto the people, and to testify that it is he which was ordained of God to be the Judge of quick and dead', Acts 10:42.

This is the witness of the Creator at the beginning of the world; it is the testimony of the Word made flesh in the midst of time; just as it will be the sentence of the great Judge at the last assize in that day when this world shall be no more.

This is the record of Almighty God from everlasting to everlasting. It is the divine and heavenly utterance of the one

9

mediator between God and men, the man Christ Jesus, in the testament which he spake whilst yet upon earth.

In him, by him, and with him, stand the great and holy men who, moved by the Holy Ghost, inspired of God, wrote the holy scriptures. All the prophets, saints, seers, apostles, the excellent of the earth, the choicest from among men, all speak with one voice. And that voice, which speaks from heaven, resonant with everlasting truth, declares to this day, 'In the beginning God created the heaven and the earth'.

However, before one can approach the early chapters of Genesis, particularly concerning the Creation, it is essential to clear the truth from the orchestrated—mark that: *orchestrated* —assault of infidels.

Such has been the propaganda initiated by, and on behalf of, the majority of those claiming to be 'scientists', followed by a host of lesser academics, whose passionate concern has been to turn every fact as if it prejudiced the real truth of divine Creation, that the world has followed after them.

In consequence, so solid appears the ephemeral fantasy of evolution, that one is obliged to pause at the threshold in order to expose the pathetically flimsy pretexts of this ungodly confederation.

The more so because the unfounded hypotheses of these people have prevailed to be incorporated into the sciences of cosmology, geology, astronomy, palaeontology, zoology, bio-chemistry, geochronology, and biology.

Such an invasion of hypothesis into the disciplines of science properly so called has not only taken over the high ground of each particular discipline, it has prevailed to bias the entire system governing the curriculum of our schools.

All this, together with the media, the newspapers, and, indeed, the film industry, causes the public to be bombarded with the taken-for-granted claims of the unproven and unprovable geological time-scale as if it were fact. The same applies to the hypothesis of evolution. But these are not facts. The truth is that they are fiction.

Nevertheless the groundless and illusory guesswork of evolutionists and uniformitarians defies the Creator, the Creation, and the solid evidence of scientific data, universally propagating their wholly speculative—but utterly ungodly—conclusions as if these fictional essays were science.

However, despite the arrogance of such claims, the almost fanatical zeal of their proponents, and the withering scorn poured upon all who dare to question them, there exists a very considerable body of scientists—true scientists—quietly presenting enough unanswered and unanswerable evidence for ever to expose the bigoted myopia of those whose strident tones have all but drowned the gentle voice of reason.

Before coming to the actual record of the Creation, I think it right to add to the testimony of those whose writings composed the holy scriptures. I quote the witness of the eminent scientists—second to none in their disciplines—who alike with one voice affirm 'In the beginning God created the heaven and the earth'.

Take for an example the testimony of Dr. A.J. Monty White, who, whilst reading for an honours degree in Chemistry, studied geology up to pass degree level. He was awarded a Ph.D. for his research in the field of Gas Kinetics.

Dr. White obtained a Science Research Council Post-doctoral Fellowship, investigating the optical and electrical properties of organic semi-conductors. Dr. White is a senior administrator at the University of Wales Institute of Science and Technology.

Consider what a scientist of such standing has to say. I refer to Dr. White's book 'What About Origins?' published by Dunestone Printers Ltd., Newton Abbot, Devon, England. I take the liberty of quoting the following momentously significant introductory paragraph of this scientist: 'The majority of people in this country have been brainwashed by the state education system and the mass media into believing that Evolution is a proven fact when in fact this is not so.'

In his book Dr. White examines the evidence for his statement from a scientist's viewpoint, first considering the Origin of the Universe. Thoroughly and conclusively each point is weighed in the balances of science, whether the origin and nature of the Universe, or its age, or the origin and age of the Solar System.

Here is a facing of the issues with a witness, and, moreover, this is achieved with the utmost probity and scientific principle. Dr. White's conclusion under this heading is devastating.

No proof whatsoever in any shape or in the least form remotely supports the generally held speculative conjectures either for the origin, nature, or age of the Universe, the Solar System, or, of course, the Earth itself.

The same scientific exactitude characterizes Dr. White's examination of the Origin of Life, drawn from the consideration of disciplines eluding most of us, such as Synthetic Chemical Evolution, D and L Amino Acids, the Formation of Proteins, Hypercycles, all of which are considered with the most objective and dispassionate scrutiny.

And with what result? This scientist concludes what is scientifically the inevitable result: 'In the beginning God created the heaven and the earth.' There is no other scientifically viable conclusion.

Again, Dr. White surges forward over all the territory to which Evolutionists have for so long laid their flimsy claims. He bursts through the gossamer web woven by atheistic bigots concerning the Origin of the Species.

He exposes the error of their conclusions regarding the age of fossils, and their nature, at once demolishing the twin pillars of their cherished shrine.

And all this he achieves in the cold light of the reality of the scientific facts. What appears is that their conclusions from these facts are nothing but unproven and unprovable theories.

The same is true of Dr. White's illuminating chapter on Dating Processes, whether of Radio Carbon Dating, Dendrochronology, Potassium-Argon Dating, or Uranium-Thorium-Lead Dating, showing that the assumptions inherent in these methods of dating the age of the earth are questionable and sometimes incorrect. Dr. White ably demonstrates that the different methods of Dating frequently contradict one another.

One of Dr. White's most telling conclusions reveals that even if—from observation—the earth were to be correctly dated back to its creation, the figure realized would in any event be excessive because of the very truth which atheistic scientists deny.

What truth is that? They fail to consider the *appearance*—the *superficial* appearance—of age *when* the earth was created. Why? They fail to consider it, because they deny the Creation in and of itself, and therefore the nature of its first appearance.

Hence by such false presuppositions they would date the earth older than can be imagined *even at the very moment in which God spoke it into existence from nothing.* Denying that Creation, they would draw false conclusions from the mere *semblance* of age at the moment of Creation.

13

Dr. White considers that as a result of co-ordinating the various scientific dating methods, the age of the earth can be calculated to be in the range of some ten thousand years. Precisely that which accords with the account of the Creation, of the early history of the Earth, and of the cataclysmic and global nature of the Flood.

At this point I would stress that it is not that I wish to give any impression of scientific knowledge. I do not. In fact of a number of the terms and disciplines I am rather ignorant. But Dr. White is not.

Moreover, whilst so erudite a scientist confirms to me *from the available facts* the truth of the Creation and its age in terms of scientific probability, fully countering the hypothesis which atheistic infidels conjure from the same facts, I wish to say with great respect to the learned Doctor, that I do not *need* this.

Why not? Because of two things. One, I have lived long enough, and listened to my elders carefully enough, to have learned beyond a peradventure one of the most significant scientific facts in history: that is, that it never takes long before one scientist contradicts another, and, at the least, comes up with a new hypothesis denying that which previously was in fashion.

Hence I repeat the words of my forefathers, my grandfathers, and my father—all of whom had more common sense, and made more money, than the whole pack of them. These words were as follows: 'Don't try and blind *me* with science.'

The second thing is this. Whilst I, for one, deeply appreciate this corroboration from the proper conclusions to the facts, such as they are, nevertheless I do not need that corroboration.

The fact that the world—the whole world, with all its systems —has wondered after the beast does not nullify the scripture.

Let God be true, but every man a liar. Will I then defy the whole world? No. But I must confess that the whole world defies God.

Whence such conviction? Not from facts, but faith.

For I did not attain to the unshakeable conviction that 'In the beginning God created the heaven and the earth', or the biblically implicit age of the earth, by any such excellent and proper interpretation of the facts put forth with scientific and pin-point accuracy by Dr. White or by the very many excellent scientists who stand where he stands.

Whence then my conviction? From the revelation of the Father, the interior quickening of the Son of God, and the witness of the Holy Ghost. This brings in the gift of God.

What gift is that? Saving faith. This is the inwardly bestowed gift of God. Nevertheless faith comes by hearing, and hearing by the word of God.

By the objective word of God the interior work of God is effected, by creating within the faith of God's elect. As to faith, this interior, divinely endued, spiritually inspiring, and inwardly illuminating candle of the Lord in the heart of his own lights up man's natural darkness.

Faith hears. Faith echoes. Let there be light: and there is light. And God reaches within by his mighty hand to separate the light from the darkness. In his light, we see light.

The page itself seems to light up to the beams of faith, and we cry, 'Through faith we understand that the worlds were framed by the word of God, so that things which are seen were not made of things which do appear', Heb. 11:3.

However the fact of such divinely given conviction does not mean that I do not endorse and recommend the scientific writings of Dr. White and his colleagues world-wide; for why should our children—or for the matter of that, the general public—be suffocated by lies?

Or why should the sheer bias of atheistic scientists juggling with such ungodly hypotheses conjured from scientific facts be presumed to have the same value and credentials as the facts themselves?

It is from the undisputed facts of scientifically verified data that speculative scientists depart, leaving the world of science in order to enter that of mere guesswork. As if it were science itself, they hypothesize their baseless—but destructively harmful —conjectures. And why should they get away with it?

Hence I commend Dr. White's first-class work.

As, for example—for I might multiply the testimony of sound scientific witnesses—I commend with equal fervour the superbly balanced presentation of Dr. Whitcomb and Professor Morris.

Here an overwhelming and convincing weight of evidence amassed from a vast array of scientific data provides the basis of their thesis under the title of 'The Genesis Flood', published by The Presbyterian and Reformed Publishing Company of Philadelphia in the United States.

It would be difficult to overstate either the academic importance of Morris and Whitcomb's work, or its outstanding contribution. Already having given time and space to reviewing the arguments presented by Dr. White, it lies beyond my present scope to summarize the complex and extensive subject matter so ably handled by Dr. Whitcomb and Professor Morris.

However, there can be no doubt whatsoever that here is an outstanding and original treatise, showing to a demonstration from the apparent age of the earth at the instant of its creation;

from the ravages of the Fall; and from the Genesis Flood itself, *the only reasonable answer to the scientific data available.*

It stands to the perpetual disgrace of the authorities of the Department of Education of the Government of the United States of America that the standard syllabus of both schools and universities was not comprehensively revised in consequence of the publication of a work the scientific implications of which placed them under immediate public obligation.

In the event the bigoted and unscientific shelving of what could not be answered reminds me of the treatment received by Dean Burgon in his 'Revision Revised', and 'The Last Twelve Verses of Mark', in an earlier era. And as then the academic world blindly followed Great Britain, so now its present equivalent trails abjectly after America.

Dr. Whitcomb and Professor Morris were undoubtedly correct. And yet in the issue that correctness was an irrelevance to a scientific, academic, and educational system pervaded by atheistic denial of the Creation, and by an ungodly rejection of the Flood.

The authors foresaw this. They introduced their work with the words 'We realize, of course, that modern scholarship will be impatient with such an approach. Our conclusions must unavoidably be coloured by our Biblical presuppositions, and this we plainly acknowledge.

'But uniformitarian scholarship is no less bound by *its* own presuppositions and these are quite as dogmatic as those of our own!

'The assumptions of historical continuity and scientific naturalism are no more susceptible of genuine scientific *proof* than are Biblical catastrophism and supernaturalism. Furthermore we believe that certain of the assumptions implicit in

17

evolutionary theory are much farther removed from scientific actualities than are our own premises.'

Whitcomb and Morris point out that the apparent age of the earth *at* creation is of necessity ignored by those who deny Creation, assuming the *then* appearance of age to be caused by nothing save the *present* processes of change and decay. Of course such baseless fancy arrives at fantastically exaggerated figures for the age of the earth!

Likewise those who deny the catastrophic effects of the universal flood—which Peter tells us destroyed '*the world* that then was'—suppose that its *year long effect* is nothing other than the consequences of the uniform and uninterrupted passage of time.

From this it follows that far from millions, a more correct estimate—and one wholly agreeable to scripture—of the age of the earth should be measured in terms of thousands of years.

Dr. Whitcomb and Professor Morris state that 'There is nothing fundamentally inviolable about even rates of *radioactive* decay'. They inform us that geologists *necessarily* leave the strict domain of *science* when they become *historical* geologists. From then on they become speculators.

The authors stress that they have no quarrel whatever with geological *science*, the disciplines of which, they say, contribute significantly to our understanding and utilization of terrestrial resources.

They continue to show that—evolutionary and uniformitarian—historical geology has not changed or developed in any essential particular for over a hundred years.

It was then that its basic philosophical structure was first worked out by such *non-geologists* as Charles Lyell (a lawyer),

William Smith (a surveyor), James Hutton (an agriculturalist), John Playfair (a mathematician), George Cuvier (a comparative anatomist), Charles Darwin (a failed divinity student), besides various motley theologians.

It needs no intellect and little stretching of the imagination to deduce what so diverse a collection of foreigners to geology actually *did* have in common. And *that* enmity against the Almighty provided the feet of clay on which the idol of evolutionary uniformitarianism totters on its path to the abyss.

The main body of Whitcomb and Morris' outstanding work simply overwhelms the reader *on the grounds of science*. Its range, depth, and exactitude make its thesis no less than stupendous, and its effect more than devastating.

After perusal of this work its opponents are left with one of two courses: either admit Whitcomb and Morris to be as revolutionary as was Galileo in his day; or adopt what amounts to no more than the same bigoted and myopic attitude of Galileo's objectors.

This time however, the prejudice rests not on the basis of the presumably flat earth, but on the ground of the denial of the existence of the Creator, of the fact of the Creation, and of the certainty of the Flood.

But the monumental opus of Whitcomb and Morris was far from ignored by a multitude of individual scientists. Although to the disgrace of mass-educational manipulators it *was* dismissed—not even being accorded the courtesy of inclusion in the syllabus on the ground of alternative scientific hypothesis—worse than dismissed, this unique presentation was *ignored* by the scientific, academic, and educational bodies.

I cannot leave this brief commendation of 'The Genesis Flood' without reference to the name and record of at least some of the vast number of its individual scientifically — not to say conscientiously—minded advocates.

For instance, a Geologist, John C. McCampbell, Ph.D., University of North Carolina, formerly on geology faculties at Rutgers and Tulane, now Professor and Head of Department of Geology, University of South Western Louisiana, states 'The authors have clearly shown that the Bible teaches a unique Creation and subsequent world-wide Deluge, and that the major facts of geology and other sciences can be satisfactorily oriented within this framework.'

Take an eminent Chemist, E.H. Hadley, Ph.D., University of Michigan, Professor of Chemistry, Southern Illinois University: 'After studying this book, I recommend it without reservation.'

Or a Geneticist. The eminent Walter E. Lammerts, Ph.D. in Genetics, University of California, affirms 'The authors clearly show that the earth's scarred surface and deeper geological structures resulted from sudden catastrophe. Uniformitarian theories of geology simply do not explain this.'

Another reference is that from an Archaeologist, Merrill F. Unger, Ph.D. 'A brilliant and compelling challenge to the theories of modern uniformitarian geology, and a desperately needed discussion on a crucial point of the alleged clash between Scripture and Science.'

Or, for example, a Geophysicist, L.A.M. Barnette, B.S. and Ch.E., Rice University, twenty-seven years in the petroleum industry, including ten years research in geophysical and stratigraphical identification techniques: 'A superb record of the indelible facts imprinted on the face of the earth by the world-wide catastrophic flood of Noah's time. Remarkably complete, well-documented, accurately analysed: truly scientific.'

This testimony might go on and on. Let it suffice to close with the witness of a Biologist, Edwin Y. Monsma, Ph.D., Professor of Biology, Calvin College: 'This book clearly shows the fallacy of the uniformitarian interpretation of past history and in so doing strikes at the very heart of evolutionary thinking.'

It must constantly be borne in mind that until comparatively recent times, both the Creation and the Deluge, besides the biblically estimated age of the earth, were all taken for granted.

What I have shown is that the radical change wrought by modern atheistic and innovative theories does not and cannot alter the testimony of the saints, the prophets, the apostles, or of the Lord Jesus Christ himself. And since these were those inspired of God, filled with the Holy Ghost, and in the latter case the very Word of God himself, this testimony can neither be broken, superseded, nor overthrown.

Furthermore on a different level I have presented the witness of a substantial number of eminent scientists, each one of whom gives the lie to evolutionary uniformitarianism.

The truth is that in the last days a blinding delusion has come upon mankind for the exceeding wickedness that covers the earth, and fills Christendom. A great part of this delusion lies in the spirit that has swept over the compulsory educational system under the falsely so called name of science, denying the Creation.

These vast changes of comparatively recent origin are nothing but the very signs preceding and leading up to the end of the world. This is the time for the people of God to take heed, abiding steadfast in the unchanged and unchangeable word of God.

The true facts of science, and the conscientious protest of true scientists, may comfort God's people, but that people

21

would do well ever to bear in mind that such things can neither beget faith, nor increase it.

Faith comes by hearing, and hearing by the word of God. And nothing else. Indeed, whilst I am impressed with the witness of these scientists over what is wrong, I am not at all impressed by their grasp of what is right. To be frank, I find most of them in a pedantic manner biblically correct, yet nevertheless painfully unspiritual.

Thus far I have observed the testimony of the Lord; of the holy men of God, who, borne along by the Holy Ghost, wrote the holy scriptures; and finally that of the apostles of our Lord Jesus Christ. To this has been added the scientific witness of conscientious and honest scientists.

Beyond reasonable doubt, this witness established the Creation; the Deluge; and the approximate age of the Earth.

This witness and testimony I have deemed to be essential *before* opening the truth of the first chapters of Genesis, particularly upon the Creation, because of the all-persuasive influence of the worldly systems of science, education, information, and entertainment.

These organised systems in the world ignore the Creator, the Creation, and the Deluge. Such essential verities are denied in favour of evolutionary uniformitarianism, which gives incredible ages of unbelievably vast eras in and to a world which is supposed perchance somehow or another to have formed itself. And they *believe* that?

This confirms that 'We know that we are of God, and the whole world lieth in wickedness', I John 5:19. It shows that 'The spirit that now worketh in the children of disobedience', Eph. 2:2, is none other than 'the god of this world', II Cor. 4:4, namely, 'The Devil, and Satan, which deceiveth the whole world', Rev. 12:9. This is why 'all the world wondered after the beast', Rev. 13:3.

Moreover it is clear that in little more than the past century, titanic forces of deception have been let loose upon a godless and willing mankind, and in an apostate and complacent church. This is the fulfilment in the latter times of what was spoken expressly by the Spirit in the beginning, that there should be a departure from the faith in consequence of the activity of seducing spirits, I Tim. 4:1.

Because of the mounting iniquity and towering godlessness manifest up to and over the past few generations, the restraints laid by Almighty God upon the degree to which the world could be deceived by the mystery of iniquity have been removed, II Thess. 2:7.

These have gone, and the mystery of iniquity—for over a century—has worked unchecked, pervading the world and its various systems more and more openly, II Thess. 2:3-10. This in turn has resulted in a blinding—and strong—delusion, that the world, and fallen religion, should believe a lie, for now it is certain that they will not receive the love of the truth, II Thess. 2:11,12.

Against such a background I am to set forth this teaching on Creation, in the will of God.

Hence, I say, before opening Genesis chapter one verse one, it is necessary first to clear the atmosphere from the pervading lies of evolutionary and uniformitarian 'scientists' whose set objective has been to argue the Creator out of Creation, Creation out of existence, and expand time until it knows neither beginning nor end.

But both inspired saints and true scientists have echoed with a witness, 'In the beginning God created the heaven and the earth'.

In concert they have shown to a demonstration that time is not eternity. Time had a beginning, and that beginning was from the Creation of the world: 'And the evening and the morning were the *first* day.'

Alike the faithful witnesses join in one to declare that time will have an end: 'Because he hath appointed a day, in the which he will judge the world in righteousness by that man whom he hath ordained.' This is called 'The *last* day'.

Of that first day and the subsequent six days, as of that last day at the end of time, the people of God have been taught by the Spirit of the living God from the very beginning.

With one voice their testimony rings from the old testament since the creation of man, to reverberate through the new testament till this present hour, so as to vibrate the chords of eternity till time shall be no more: 'In the beginning God created the heaven and the earth.'

'For ask now of the days that are past, which were before thee, since the day that God created man upon the earth, and ask from the one side of heaven unto the other, whether there hath been any such thing as this great thing is, or hath been heard like it?'

'For in six days the LORD made heaven and earth, the sea, and all that in them is, and rested the seventh day: wherefore the LORD blessed the sabbath day, and hallowed it.'

Blessed and hallowed? But what do atheists; what do evolutionists; what do uniformitarians; what do any who deny the works of the LORD, his mighty acts, and his wondrous deeds; say, what do these know of the blessing? what do they know of what is hallowed?

How can they know anything, who despise everything, and believe nothing? Theirs is not the blessing, and hence they must be under the curse. Not for them what is hallowed: there-fore they remain defiled. The blessing is for faith, not works, for works are abominable in the sight of God. But he that is of faith is blessed, and blessed to hear the fruitful word.

'Thus saith God the LORD, he that created the heavens, and stretched them out; he that spread forth the earth, and that which cometh out of it; he that giveth breath unto the people upon it, and spirit to them that walk therein.'

So the prophet Isaiah wrote, who without controversy fore-saw the broad sweeps of time far into the distant future. He spake forth history before the event. Isaiah predicted the minutest details centuries in advance of their taking place.

And will mere self-styled *scientists* contend with such a towering figure as Isaiah, and rise up in their petty transient folly against his massive and abiding wisdom? Is it for this that God the LORD gave them breath?

Did ever the Almighty breathe into them the spirit of prophecy, or set within their souls the candle of his wisdom, that they should dispute with the prophet in whom these things actually did take place? Have they not heard? Do they not know?

Have they never heard the questionings of those of old, more prudent than themselves, namely, Where is the wise? where is the scribe? where is the disputer of this world? hath not God made foolish the wisdom of this world? For after that in the wisdom of God the world by wisdom knew not God, it pleased God by the foolishness of preaching to save them that believe.

And do they yet disbelieve? Be astonished, O heavens, at this. O earth, earth, earth, hear the word of the LORD: 'I have made the earth, and created man upon it; I, even my hands, have stretched out the heavens, and all their host have I commanded.'

25

'For thus saith the LORD that created the heavens; God himself that formed the earth and made it; he hath established it, he created it not in vain, he formed it to be inhabited: I am the LORD; and there is none else.'

Then shall the thing formed say to him that formed it, Get thee hence? Shall the breath of the creature be spent in its passing moment, expiring even as it breathes to the Creator, Thou art not?

The psalmist testifies on another wise, saying, LORD, thou hast been our dwelling place in all generations. Before the mountains were brought forth, or ever thou hadst formed the earth and the world, even from everlasting to everlasting, thou art God.

Then who are these silly, blind men, frail as an autumn leaf? 'The lofty looks of man shall be humbled, and the haughtiness of men shall be bowed down, and the LORD alone shall be exalted in that day.'

'For the day of the LORD of hosts shall be upon every one that is proud and lofty, and upon every one that is lifted up; and he shall be brought low.' 'Cease ye from man, whose breath is in his nostrils: for wherein is he to be accounted of?'

Let them take heed therefore to the wise man, who counselled, 'Remember now thy Creator in the days of thy youth'. Hast thou not known? hast thou not heard, that the everlasting God, the LORD, the Creator of the ends of the earth, fainteth not, neither is weary? there is no searching of his understanding.

No less an authority than the Holy Ghost in the gospel according to Mark records the very words of Jesus Christ, the Son of God: 'From the beginning of the creation God made them male and female', Mk. 10:6.

If so, not only was the eternal Son *at* the Creation; but by him God performed the work. 'My Father worketh hitherto, and I work.'

But where were these creatures of a day, whose audacious premise is the denial of God from everlasting to everlasting? They were not there; yet this does not prevent their futile works from springing out of the puerile thesis that he who created all things by Jesus Christ has no more reality than that which he himself had created and made in six days.

Yet for all their vaunting and boasting, for all their airs of detachment and supercilious criticism, upon them shall come to pass the words of Jesus, Mark 13:19, 'For in those days shall be affliction, such as was not from the beginning of the creation which God created unto this time, neither shall be.' And where then shall they appear?

For these are they that serve the creature more than the Creator, Rom. 1:25. And why, if not to boast in themselves? But where shall their boasting appear, when, impaled upon the fiery sword, they find in the day of judgment that their quest for knowledge probed a path forbidden to Adam and his posterity?

The truth is that Christ is the wisdom of God. In him are hid all the treasures of wisdom and knowledge. He that cometh to him he shall not cast out.

But whoso taketh of the tree of the knowledge of good and evil, or seeks the path to that tree, shall find a flaming sword turning every way, to keep the way to the tree of life. No life is from the quarter which is sought by those who are dead even while they think that they live.

Life is in God's favour. That is, by grace through faith. And so it was set forth in the beginning, for 'By him were all things created, that are in heaven, and that are in earth, visible and invisible, whether they be thrones, or dominions, or principalities, or powers: all things were created by him, and for him: and he is before all things, and by him all things consist', Colossians 1:16,17.

And what then shall we say to these things? 'Thou art worthy, O Lord, to receive glory and honour and power: for thou hast created all things, and for thy pleasure they are and were created.'

Let all men, even these men, therefore take heed. For a man of God holier than they could imagine, and with vision beyond their conception, bears witness against them.

'And the angel which I saw stand upon the sea and upon the earth lifted up his hand to heaven, and sware by him that liveth for ever and ever, who created heaven, and the things that therein are, and the earth, and the things that therein are, and the sea, and the things which are therein, that there should be time no longer', Revelation 10:5,6.

This prophetic vision ushers in the consummation of that which was brought into being on the first day.

When time shall be no more, when the last day shall have come to pass, take notice, then, then there shall be no question, but only astonishment, confusion of face, and a confounding of the gainsayer, to discover of a truth, too late, that 'In the beginning *God* created the heaven and the earth', Genesis 1:1.

II

Creation: The ELOHIM Account

THE first book of Moses, called Genesis, gives all the knowledge of the Creation of the world, and of man, that is necessary for the good of humanity.

Anything further, or any probings beyond this revelation, far from being for man's good, in practice result in a relentless slide down the slippery slope of unbelief. This takes the mind of the doubter in an ever increasing departure from the Creator to be absorbed with the creature.

Indeed, as comparatively recent history shows, such restless curiosity not only robs men of the knowledge of God, it steals from them the last vestige of desire for that knowledge. In place of this there is a fascination with so-called 'scientific' attainment, which—for all its apparent gains—has as a whole taken man to the brink of destruction, both for himself, the creature, the environment, and the world itself.

No matter how men may twist and turn, scoff or mock, these are concrete and evident facts which stare humanity in the face. The only antidote to this lies in the fear of God, so as to be content—as were our fathers—with that sufficient knowledge which it has pleased the Almighty to reveal in his holy word.

On opening the book of Genesis perhaps the most remarkable feature to strike the reader is that there are *two* records of the Creation, not one. These differ immensely, not only in emphasis and direction but also in volume and form. The reason is spiritual, and no one can attain to the understanding of the Creation without that spiritual knowledge.

Said Jesus, Moses wrote of me. And again he saith, O fools, and slow of heart to believe all that the prophets have spoken. Note that: *All* that the prophets have spoken. '*And beginning at Moses* and all the prophets, he expounded unto them in *all* the scriptures the things concerning himself.'

Do not think that Jesus' exposition excluded the Creation. How could it? It began at Moses. And Moses begins 'In the beginning God created the heaven and the earth.' But save that Christ expounds the first chapters of Genesis, they remain as dark as night to the reader. When God says 'Let there be light', then all becomes radiant. But not until then.

For God, who commanded the light to shine out of darkness, hath shined in our hearts, to give the light of the knowledge of the glory of God in the face of Jesus Christ. In that light we see light. But not without that light. Without that light, darkness is upon the face of the deep of the soul, and nothing of the Creation is discernible.

You see that a preceding interior work of illumination is needed to get at the spiritual record—or, rather, records—of the Creation. Such a work, called 'The spirit of wisdom and revelation in the knowledge of him', comes from God in Christ: 'Then opened he their understanding, that they might understand the scriptures.'

For the truth is that hidden in the records of the Creation, lies the revelation of Jesus Christ, quite apart from the record of Adam. Nor ought this to surprise the reader. For Christ is he in whom are hid *all* the treasures of wisdom and knowledge, Col. 2:3. And if so, the treasures in the first chapters of Genesis.

Hence Peter affirms that the prophets, 'Prophesied of the grace that should come unto you: searching what, or what manner of time the Spirit of Christ which was in them did signify, when it testified beforehand the sufferings of Christ, and the glory that should follow', I Pet. 1:10.

And again Peter speaks of Christ 'As of a lamb without blemish and without spot: who verily was foreordained *before the foundation of the world*', I Pet. 1:19,20. And if foreordained before the foundation of the world, it is hardly likely that when that world was founded, no mention of him should be made. But it *was* made. Only, it was hidden.

Hence Jesus speaks of 'Things kept secret from the foundation of the world', Mt. 13:35, and in another place of a kingdom prepared for his sheep—but not for any goats—from the foundation of the world, to be entered into when this world is no more, Mt. 24:34.

Known unto God are all his works from the beginning of the world. Moreover, also known of him are all his purposes from before the foundation of the world. Then it is hardly likely that these will not be revealed in a hidden mystery at the Creation of the world.

Purposes before the Creation of the world? 'According as he hath chosen us in him before the foundation of the world', Eph. 1:4. So Titus speaks of the hope of eternal life, which God, that cannot lie, promised before the world began, Titus 1:2.

Likewise II Tim. 1:9 tells us that God 'hath saved us, and called us with an holy calling, not according to our works, but according to his own purpose and grace, which was given us in Christ Jesus before the world began.' And will anyone tell me that this was not mysteriously signified in the Creation when the world did begin?

31

How can anyone so speak? They cannot, because, Eph. 3:9, 'The fellowship of the mystery, which from the beginning of the world hath been hid in God, who created all things by Jesus Christ', was signified by figure, type, and prophecy since the world began.

Hence Rev. 13:8 speaks of 'the Lamb slain from the foundation of the world.' Rev. 17:8 refers to names written in the book of life from the foundation of the world. And Rom. 16:25 declares that Paul's gospel, and the preaching of Jesus Christ, are both according to the revelation of the mystery kept secret since the world began. Secret, yes. But secretly signified by signs, figures of the true, and shadows of the reality yet to come. And, at that, as early as Genesis chapters 1 and 2.

For the first Creation heralded the second. And the first Adam prefigured the last. Says John of the end of the world, 'And I saw a new heaven and a new earth: for the first heaven and the first earth were passed away', Rev. 21:1.

Thus declares Paul, 'And so it is written'—written where? Paul *actually quotes Genesis 2:7*. Written *there*—'The first man Adam was made a living soul; the last Adam was made a quickening spirit.' If so, these are mysteries signified at the beginning of Genesis.

Now, if the new testament reveals that there is to be a new Creation when this present world has passed away; and if the apostles' doctrine declares that there is a first Adam and a last, a first man and a second; and if these things were determined before the foundation of the world, tell me, Is it likely that *two* records of the Creation, and *two* accounts of the forming of man in Genesis provide no more than a mere coincidence?

The truth is that in the purpose and counsel of God there *are* two Creations; there *are* two men; and there *are* two seeds.

This was determined before the foundation of the world and the creation of Adam. And it will be consummated when this world is no more in the resurrection of life from the dead. Then is it possible that no hint, no unfolding, no figure of these things existed in the beginning?

At the least, therefore, it follows that one ought seriously to consider the comparison between the two records of the Creation, the first from Genesis 1:1 to 2:3, and the second following on in chapter 2:4. Why two accounts? and what is the difference between them?

The fact that within so small a compass there *are* two accounts of Creation, with such vastly different emphases, *must* indicate a *spiritual* meaning indicative of a revelation—then hidden—of things yet to come.

If so, the *fact* of the Creation of the heaven and the earth, and the *fact* of the creation of man, are stressed *again* in Genesis in order to point to the truth that neither the first Creation nor the first man answer to the hidden mystery of God's eternal purpose. They but *point* to that purpose.

And so it is written at the last, And I saw a *new* heaven and a *new* earth: for the *first* heaven and the *first* earth were passed away. And again, But the heavens and the earth which *are now* are kept in store. That is, kept in store until the bringing in of the new.

Likewise, there is a first Adam and *his* seed or posterity; and there is a *last* Adam with *his* seed and *his* posterity. Of that last Adam, which is Christ, the first Adam in the garden was called 'the figure of him that was to come', Rom. 5:14. But if a figure, *Where is that figure but in Genesis?* And if two accounts appear, *Why but for this same reason?*

In the beginning obviously there was but *one* Creation, for which but *one* record would have sufficed. But in the fore-knowledge and counsel of God *another Creation was yet to come.* Likewise in the beginning but one man appeared. But in the eternal purpose of God *another Man was yet to come.* This hidden mystery, kept secret from the foundation of the world, *was signified in a hidden way from the very beginning.*

That is why there are two accounts. That is why the two records are written in such different ways. Because aspects are included and excluded respectively to stress *the difference between what was in Adam and this Creation, and what would be in Christ and the new Creation.* Why? Because *two men, and their seeds respectively*, were in view *from the very beginning.*

The *first* account, Genesis 1:1 to 2:3, reveals the *vision of* Creation. So that the record answers to Creation as God envisaged it in terms of his eternal purpose. Of course, the narrative records what really happened, but *the way in which that narrative is written* stresses the divine vision in and of itself.

Now, *that* vision is not for *this* Creation, although it is drawn from the facts of this Creation. Nevertheless the Holy Ghost so words it—emphasizing one thing and ignoring another— that the first Creation was made to prefigure the last. In a word 'the figure' of that to come.

This is what is in view: *first* there was divine purpose, the realization of which would be in the new heaven and the new earth, a Creation suited for the last Adam, the second man, and his seed and posterity. The first Creation *reflected* that, and the first *account* of that Creation signified it.

Hence in the first account certain things are missing, apparent in the second account. For example, the name JEHOVAH is missing. In the first record of Creation it is a question of ELOHIM. This occurs thirty-three times. It is a plural name.

In the Hebrew idiom plurality *may* stress nothing save force and power, but in the Spirit *the plural allows for the coming revelation of Father, Son, and Holy Ghost.* The name JEHOVAH, however, does not. But then that name occurs only in the second account. It does not occur in the first.

Other things are missing from the first record, present in the second. Not only the name JEHOVAH, but the name Adam. The dust—or ground—from which Adam was formed does not appear in the first account.

The word Soul is missing. But it must be missing if the first and not the second account was used to indicate the promise of Christ. 'The first man Adam was made a living soul', Paul states, 'and so it is written.' Written, that is, not in the first but in the second account in Genesis.

Further observe that in the first record of Creation in Genesis the Garden of Eden is not mentioned. The tree of life does not appear. Neither is there any reference to the tree of the knowledge of good and evil, much less the serpent or the Fall. These things do not belong to the ELOHIM account. They belong to the second, the JEHOVAH Elohim account, commencing at Genesis 2:4.

Although the dawning *promise* of the coming of Christ mysteriously appeared in the first—the ELOHIM—account of Creation in Genesis, in fact Christ himself in person, made manifest in the flesh, was not to appear until aeons later. Neither shall the *new* Creation—prefigured by the old—be made manifest until after the last day of this present world.

So that the *shadow* of Christ in *this* Creation, preceded the *substance* of his coming, just as the first — or old — Creation heralded the certainty of *that new Creation* which is yet to come.

35

And so it is written, The first man Adam was made a living soul; the last Adam was made a quickening spirit. Howbeit that was not first which is spiritual, but that which is natural; and afterward that which is spiritual. The first man is of the earth, earthy: the second man is the Lord from heaven, I Cor. 15:45-47. And again, 'I saw a new heaven and a new earth: for the first heaven and the first earth were passed away', Rev. 21:1.

Throughout the first record of the Creation, from Genesis 1:1 to 2:3, consistently the English rendering for the Hebrew ELOHIM is God. The name God occurs thirty-three times in this passage.

When it comes to the second account of Creation, commencing at Genesis 2:4 there is a change in the divine name. It is an addition. To ELOHIM is added the name JEHOVAH. This has been translated LORD God in the English bible. But what is the significance of these things?

The first name to be used—and used singly and exclusively in the opening record—refers to God absolutely. The second is more specific. In this case the name God is still there, ELOHIM is retained, but to it is added the title of JEHOVAH. It is still God but it is God *in that covenant name*. Now, a *covenant* name means that God *reveals* himself in a certain way—in this case a *legal* way—to a chosen people, namely Israel.

This means that there is a revelation of himself. Not just God. Not absolutely ELOHIM. But JEHOVAH Elohim. The LORD God. It is the beginning of disclosure under the old testament.

At first—and if first, then at the beginning—God's name is absolute: there is no disclosure. In such a case the mystery of deity *remains* undisclosed. With the addition of JEHOVAH—LORD God—in Genesis 2:4, the disclosure to Israel of him who was to give the law under the old covenant commences.

The very wording of the first account of what happened at the Creation is framed so as to intimate the vision in the mind of God of and for his Son in the new testament *first*. Of necessity this account does not reveal God—ELOHIM—it demonstrates that there is *an unrevealed mystery*, hidden in the Godhead, absolute and inscrutable.

In the second account *that detail which was deliberately omitted from the first record now comes in, and it comes in under the name LORD God.* JEHOVAH Elohim. Here he begins to be made known as the lawgiver under the old covenant, because here the *reality* of what took place in Adam of necessity evokes divine response, which in turn reveals his character.

But the name ELOHIM — translated God — used exclusively throughout the opening record of the Creation—Genesis 1:1 to 2:3—tells the reader little or nothing about the nature of God in himself. It is an absolute term. There is nothing to be said beyond this, because nothing is revealed beyond it. Nothing appears but the obvious, namely, his divine self-existence.

Absolutely, inscrutably, ELOHIM is the term for God. The Hebrew is in the plural. The use of the plural is not restricted to number: in Hebrew idiom it can be indicative of force or power.

Maybe so, but it is *also* indicative of plurality, and I think it absurdly pedestrian to rule out the presence of a gentle, spiritual indication that God absolutely, yet to be revealed in a mystery, should in the fulness of time be made known as one God in three Persons: Father, Son, and Holy Ghost.

However in terms of ELOHIM everything was unknown. Nothing was revealed of his *person*, save the absolute and unquestioned assertion of his being, and the *fait accompli* of his acts. He exists and he creates. He is God and he does that.

Of course this manifests supernatural and infinite power beyond imagination, let alone comprehension. But it is not a question of imagination or comprehension. It is a matter of fact; it is a cause of worship; and it is the genesis of faith. Anything less, or whatever to the contrary, is at once the evil of godlessness and the quintessence of irrationality.

For all that, the mystery of the divine nature—that is, how ELOHIM appears in and of himself—is not revealed in this account of the Creation. Nevertheless the fact that *he* did *that*, and did it *in this way*, namely, that he did *create*, and created in this order and at that time, shows things about him not otherwise manifested. What he did does not show *him*: what he did shows things about him.

His existence is clear, his eternity is obvious. Whatever further revelation he should make of his intrinsic being and nature, can add nothing to the manifestation in Creation of God's everlasting existence, his eternal being, and his omnipotent power.

Not to recognize this, nor to worship because of it, is to fall under the condemnation of the reprobate heathen: 'Because that, when they knew God, they glorified him not as God, neither were thankful', Rom. 1:21.

The truth that the first chapter of Genesis does not reveal *who or what God is within himself* cannot disoblige men, all men everywhere, of infinite obligation. No amount of Christian revelation can ever exonerate those who profess Christ from this infinite obligation, much less reduce the awesome reverence inherent *in the very idea of God, and in the very nature of the Creation.*

God is: he is of power to form the Creation from nothing: this is the power of the Godhead: it is eternal power.

Failure under either old or new testaments to fulfil constantly and consistently the unceasing obligation and duty of reverential worship therefore is to sin against God beyond belief: 'For the invisible things of him from the creation of the world are clearly seen, being understood by the things that are made, *even his eternal power and Godhead'*, Rom. 1:20.

For all these things, neither the name God nor the fact of Creation in Genesis 1 brings in—though they *promise*—the revelation of the divine *person*. But they *do* manifest his eternity; his omnipotence; and the *fact* of his Godhead. The inscrutable God—ELOHIM—*created. What* he did, shows all that then could be seen.

His *works* proclaim him in Genesis 1. But proclaim *whom?* The revelation of whom awaited events and aeons then passing knowledge.

Nevertheless hidden in a mystery by the Holy Ghost throughout this passage, that future revelation of Christ and the world to come not only subsisted under the faintest of signs and figures, but in fact *the very existence of the distinct and unique first account of Creation in Genesis—to be followed by another—was the broadest spiritual hint of all.*

The record of the Creation in six days, and God's rest upon the seventh, occupies the whole of the first chapter and the first three verses of the second. Each evening begins the work of God, and each morning ends it. The morning brings to light what God had wrought through the darkness of the night so as to manifest a new, higher state than that which had been in existence before.

This work of God through six days, and his cessation from the completed activity on the seventh, appears under a tenfold — complete — divine manifestation. God created; God said; God saw; God divided; God called; God made; God blessed; God ended; God rested; and God sanctified.

On the six days which brought to light the work of God with the new morning, God having wrought between the previous evening and the following morning, the Hebrew repeats on each successive and progressive occasion 'And there was evening and there was morning' followed by 'the first day' through to 'the sixth day'.

This does not occur on the seventh day. On the seventh day the heavens—note the plural—and the earth were finished, and all the host of them. God had ended his work, and he rested. He does not work through the night, there is no mention of evening and morning, the seventh day. All that he willed to bring to light had come to light. Everything had come to light in six days. There was nothing for the seventh day but to rest in the light of Creation.

A great deal of speculation has existed concerning the first day. As though that day did not begin when, verse 1, 'In the beginning God created the heaven and the earth', and end at the conclusion of verse 5, 'And the evening and the morning were the first day'.

In this devious wresting of the scriptures, not only do its proponents separate the first two verses from the last three of Genesis 1:1-5, but they invent the most incredible fantasies which they thrust into the rent which they have torn in the account of the first day. And why do they do this? And when did this speculation arise?

It arose at much the same time as the hypotheses of so-called 'historical geologists' took the fancy of the academic world, postulating incredible aeons for their unproved and unprovable notions of the age of the earth.

Absurdly running around in circles, they proposed to 'prove' the age of the strata of the earth by the fossils found in each layer respectively. But how to 'prove' the age of the fossils? Ah, by the strata, of course. So who are the fossils?

Nevertheless the craze of godless uniformitarian hypotheses took the world by storm, the theologians and divinity faculties by surprise, and self-opinionated brethren in their own conceits. Intent on flattering the academic authority, these apostates found a way of accommodating the world's opinions. How? By breaking the scripture in half between Genesis 1:2 and 1:3. But the scripture, said Jesus, cannot be broken.

Into this abominable rupture which these infidels had torn, they thrust as many millions—or billions; What did it matter? —of years as the avowedly atheistic uniformitarian evolutionists required. Dusting their hands, they completed this abomination by christening it 'The Gap'. But the gap is between their ears, and the rent is between them and the faith once delivered unto the saints.

The unspeakable errors and delusions which followed upon their wresting of the scripture in Gen. 1:2, 'And the earth *was* without form and void', which, contrary to every rule of translation they twisted into 'And the earth *became* without form and void', I flatly refuse to utter. Let their vile inventions perish with them: they shall find no utterance from my mouth; no stroke from my pen; and no place in my being.

It is important to realize that Genesis 1:1 to 2:3 is not an *explanation* of the Creation. It cannot be explained. In *that* sense this passage is not even an *account* of the Creation. God giveth no account of his matters. It is all to *purpose*, and, God being a Spirit, *spiritual* purpose. In no sense whatsoever is it educational information.

But that being given, and the simplicity and restraint of what is said concerning each successive day being received as the sum of the revelation intended, it is still true that no scientific discovery can contradict the *facts* upon which the spiritual truths conveyed by Genesis 1:1 to 2:3 are based.

41

The truth of the revelation transcends the facts, but it is founded on them. If any so-called scientific discoveries contradict either fact or foundation, then that in itself is scientific evidence that such 'discoveries' are nothing more than mere hypotheses, differing only in form from the superstitions of infidels and godless heathen.

The truth is that the prevailing majority of these so-called 'scientists' are sheer bigots, ready to believe anything and everything denigrating to the Creator and the Creation.

This was evident in a former day with the triumphant discovery of the Piltdown Man, an evolutionary wonder of wonders to 'science' and 'scientists', providing the 'missing link' between man and the apes. The skull, excavated in England in 1912, later proved to be nothing but a modern human cranium to which was welded the jaw-bone of an orang-utan.

But it was not the infatuated 'scientists' who proved it to be a fake. 'Science' could not bear to part with its darling. What happened was that finally the prankster students who manufactured and planted this fabrication confessed to their hoax, alarmed at the tumultuous and universal acclaim which had greeted such a longed-for and welcome 'proof' of the unquestionable scientific basis of evolutionists.

However it is essential — but essential — for faith to abide within the bulwarks of scripture, and this is never more true than in the case of Genesis 1:1 to 2:3. Or, to focus even more precisely, Genesis 1:1-5.

Whatever may appear in the revelation of the new testament concerning spiritual wickedness in heavenly places, the faithful will rightly divide the word of truth, concluding from the account in Genesis *no more and no less* than what is written, in the way in which it is written.

The saints will abominate speculation. They will receive revelation. They will refuse the mixing of passages in order to insert the thin end of the wedge of error. They will observe and adhere to the observation that in Genesis 1:1 to 2:3 in general, and 1:1-5 in particular, there is a restraint on the part of the Holy Ghost, without submission to which his inspiration will be sought in vain.

In this passage there is an obvious *refusal* of the Spirit to speak of things and beings invisible. There is nothing of invisible and spiritual thrones, dominions, principalities, or powers. No cognizance whatsoever is taken of angels, archangels, cherubim, or seraphim, in the account of Creation in Genesis.

In Genesis 1:1 to 2:3 nothing is said of Satan, of his fall, of his drawing a host after him, of evil angels, or of any suchlike things. *To intrude these matters into this passage therefore is unbelieving speculation, idle meandering, and must of necessity result in spiritual damage to the soul.* Faith stops up the well's mouth of such offensive pollution, obnoxious to the Holy Ghost.

Colossians 2:3 assures us that it is in Christ that all the treasures of wisdom and knowledge are hid, not in Adam. Nor are *hidden* things—such as the promise in Genesis chapter 1 of him that was to come—to be imposed upon, as a result of later revelation *beyond the scope of that given in Genesis*. Hence the apostle adds, 'And this I say, lest any man should beguile you with enticing words', Col. 2:4.

Genesis 1:1 to 2:3 is a revelation that is for *man*. Indeed, it centres upon God's creation of and purpose for man. Only, it is the promised Man, albeit the facts of the first Creation and the first man are utilized as the basis for this wonderful foreshadowing by the Holy Ghost. Everything centres upon that Man.

To bring in things about angels, speculations regarding Satan, conceits concerning the origins of evil, is to dash in

43

pieces the fragility and refinement of an account in which the Holy Ghost took such pains *to rule out speculations*. To despise this is to do despite to the Spirit of grace.

Audacious upstarts who do such things, desperate for attention, are spoken of individually and particularly by the apostle over this very matter: 'Intruding into those things which he hath not seen, vainly puffed up by his fleshly mind', Col. 2:18.

Genesis 1:1 to 2:3 is a question of man, and what is revealed in connection with man. A question? This question: 'What *is* man, that thou art mindful of him?'. The answer to that which is posed in Psalm 8, over Genesis 1, is found in Hebrews 2:6-9. And that answer is not the first, but the second Man.

So the wise will curb themselves, lest they grieve the Spirit, sent to glorify Christ. They will eschew the conjectures of carnal impostors—uncalled and unsent—who base their meanderings in Genesis 1:1-5 on passages nothing to do with the matter in question, and which the Holy Ghost keeps apart.

They conjure their abuse from such places as Isaiah 14:12— in fact a prophecy against the king of Babylon, however soaring the imagery — and Ezekiel 28:13-15 — actually in context a lamentation upon the king of Tyrus, no matter in what mystical and poetical language it may be couched.

The spiritual will never pry. Should they, they would cease to be spiritual. They will never ape the carnal and unmortified, who in their pride would transfer such passages from Isaiah or Ezekiel to force open a gap in Genesis, into which they then pour out all manner of filthy imaginings spewed forth from their pernicious and fleshly minds.

The meek and submissive mind characteristic of the spiritual humbly subdues all such high imagination, bringing every thought into captivity to the obedience of Christ.

Of Christ, yes, both in his own words and those given through his apostles: 'Beware lest any man spoil you through philosophy and vain deceit, after the tradition of men, after the rudiments of the world, and not after Christ', Col. 2:8.

Given this solemn warning, the spiritual are the more careful to confine themselves within the bounds set by the Holy Ghost in scripture. This applies to the testimony of the Creator and the Creation. There is no going beyond the text and context of the revelation itself, except to receive any explicit comment or elucidation from the new testament on Genesis 1:1 to 2:3.

And there are such comments. For example, 'In the beginning was the Word, and the Word was with God, and the Word was God. The same was in the beginning with God. All things were made by him; and without him was not anything made that was made', Jn. 1:1-3.

Here is explicit comment and clear elucidation further to Genesis 1:1, 'In the beginning God created the heaven and the earth'.

By Moses the Holy Ghost declares the Word in the beginning. But who he was, and what was the mystery of God, and of the Father, and of Christ, the Spirit does not reveal until 'The Word was made flesh, and dwelt among us, (and we beheld his glory, the glory as of the only begotten of the Father,) full of grace and truth', Jn. 1:14.

Then, and not until then, the mystery was revealed. In the beginning the nature of the Godhead remained veiled and inscrutable under the divine name ELOHIM. Nevertheless the faintest dawning rays of prophetic revelation hinted at the glory to come with the promise of the Man of God's purpose.

This in itself appeared in the manifestation of the plurality in oneness of ELOHIM: of his Spirit: and of that Word which was in the beginning, for whose coming the ages were to wait.

By him were all things created, and without him was nothing made that was made. And so it is written, 'In the beginning God created the heaven and the earth.'

It may be objected, If God created the heaven and the earth on the first day, Gen. 1:1, how can it be said that the heaven was brought into existence on the second day, Genesis 1:6-8, 'And God called the firmament Heaven. And the evening and the morning were the second day', Gen. 1:8?

This is easily answered from the words of the son of David, king Solomon, at the dedication of the temple of God, 'But who is able to build him an house, seeing the heaven and heaven of heavens cannot contain him?', II Chron. 2:6.

Here the wise man perceived from the Creation what foolish men do not: instead of cavilling at an imagined contradiction between two verses in Genesis, Solomon understood that there were not merely two, but at least three heavens—'the heaven *of heavens*'—the sum of which could not contain God.

Likewise David his father understood Moses to mean this, for by the Holy Ghost he follows Genesis over the first two days of Creation, commenting, 'The heaven, even the heavens, are the LORD's', Psalm 115:16.

To come to a conclusion, the apostle Paul states that he knew a man in Christ who was 'Caught up to the third heaven', II Cor. 12:2. And had the originators of such puerile objections experienced the same thing, it would have saved us the labour of answering their querulous trifling.

Although Genesis 1:1 states that 'In the beginning God created the heaven and the earth', yet the next verse declares, 'And the earth was without form, and void; and darkness was upon the face of the deep. And the Spirit of God moved upon the face of the waters.'

46

This seems strange. Yet not unique to the first day. For it is a truth to be observed that on *each* successive day of Creation, *a prior state existed which in consequence of the work of God on the following evening and the morning elevated the entire Creation to an increasingly advanced form.*

In that case, there is nothing surprising in the truth that the commencement of the work of God in Creation on the first day, Gen. 1:1,2, was *in anticipation of its being in divine enhancement at the conclusion of that evening and the morning,* Gen. 1:5.

This sets before us a constant principle, manifest in progressive development from each state on the previous day, to another on the next day, until, at last, 'It was very good', and God 'rested from all his work which he had created and made', Gen. 2:3.

It is necessary to observe that there is also that about Genesis chapter 1 which gives the merest hint — no more, and not a word of explanation — of another element.

Firstly, '*darkness* was upon the face of the deep.' Secondly, 'God *divided* the light from the darkness', Gen. 1:4.

Again, his command was to '*divide* the day from the night'; and 'to *divide* the light from the darkness', Gen. 1:14,18. Here things are separated not only because of their incompatibility, but also on account of their downright antipathy.

Thirdly, seven times over—the last being superlative—God pronounced 'It was good'. But the darkness was not good.

And it is a remarkable factor that whilst 'it was good' was declared on the first day, twice on the third day, once on the fourth day, once again on the fifth day, and twice on the sixth day—a sevenfold perfection of goodness in the days of Creation—*yet nothing good is said of that which concerned the second day.*

I do not comment on these things: I observe them. They are bare hints; the Spirit proceeds no further. God forbid I should advance so much as one single thought beyond the barriers set up by the Holy Ghost. On the contrary, I have reiterated the dire apostolic warnings against speculation above what is written.

It is one thing to see interpretation and revelation in the new testament on things in the old. It is another thing to go beyond the spiritual intent to which both the old testament passages and the new testament interpretations minister.

More than enough of the Holy Ghost, and revelations abundant, stand in the things written aforetime for our instruction in Genesis 1:1 to 2:3, without throwing off restraint, putting on conceit, inflating the old man, grieving the Spirit, and all for the purpose of making a fair show in the flesh.

After the Creation on the first day there was the heaven and there was the earth. As to the earth it was without form and void. There was a deep, and there were waters. The deep had a face and the waters had a face. Darkness was upon the face of the one and the Spirit of God hovered upon the face of the other.

'And God said, Let there be light: and there was light', Gen. 1:3. These were words which God spake, and he spake them by the Word.

And the Word was with God, and the Word was God. Without him was not anything made that was made.

But the light was not made, neither was it created. God said, Let there *be* light. He did not *form* it: he commanded what was self-existent to shine. 'And God saw the light, that it was good.'

As to the created heavens and earth—which was without form and void—and as to the face of the deep, and the face of the waters, one thing is certain: upon them there was no light; only darkness: albeit the Spirit of God moved upon the face of the waters. 'And God said, Let there be light: and there was light.'

Let there *be* light. That is, *there*. There is no question of God creating light. It was a matter *of bringing in the light*. That light *was*: but it was not *there*. Then God spake, and light *was* there.

Now, *God* is light, I Jn. 1:5, and in him is no darkness at all. His Spirit was there, hovering, moving. But when the Word came, his *presence* was there, who is called *The True Light*, Jn. 1:9.

When God said, Let there be light, then the Word came, the light shone, and *his presence* was *there*, who is called 'the true light', which 'now shineth'. And God saw the light, that it was good. And the light shineth in the darkness; and the darkness comprehended it not.

And God divided the light from the darkness. And God called the light Day, and the darkness he called Night. God divided, he separated, he excluded the one from the other, he put apart, by his very nature he put apart, things that were intrinsically, inalienably, and perpetually contrary and incompatible.

And, separating them, God put each in its place, never to cross the great gulf fixed by his everlasting division. Then he named each. He gave them their character by name. Light belongs to Day. Darkness belongs to Night. And there was evening and there was morning, the first day.

Momentous and unalterable divine principles have already been manifested and established. And established for ever, being founded in the necessity of God's immutable character. These things will *always* be so.

Observe that darkness and light, day and night, existed *irrespective of the sun*. The sun was not made until the fourth day. This was the first day. *God* is light. Of this the sun merely gave a faded form, a pale witness for man from the heavens.

Light is not dependent on sun, stars, heat, or burning, *as appearances seem to indicate*. Outside appearances, beyond what is visible, in a heavens above all comprehension, in dimensions past every imagination, there dwells in and one with ELOHIM that same light which began to shine *in Creation* on the first day.

The true light, which shone on the first day, lies beyond any visible or material source. That is, any *created* source. Of course it does: 'Things which are seen were not made of things which do appear', Heb. 11:3.

But the sun appears; stars are seen. Burning matter appears; artificial light is seen. But all this is nothing save the faintest glimmer from the hand of the Creator who made the things which are seen from things which do not appear: in a word, made them from nothing by his own eternal power.

Now *he*—the Creator—is *himself* light. 'God is light', I Jn. 1:5. He covereth himself with light as with a garment, Ps. 104:2. 'Who only hath immortality, dwelling in the light which no man can approach unto; whom no man hath seen, nor can see: to whom be honour and power everlasting. Amen', I Tim. 6:16.

The fact that he *dwells* in light unapproachable does not mean that his presence is not all-pervading: it is. But his *dwelling* —in dimensions incomprehensible to man—is above the heaven of heavens.

The fact that no man hath seen nor can see the deity—who dwells in light unapproachable—does not nullify the reality of the matter: it only emphasizes the absoluteness of the subsequent withdrawal of the Creator's presence from the Creation. It shows up the blackness of darkness into which mankind fell in the inward state of his heart.

Nevertheless, to those to whom God chose to do so, the light which shone on the first day *was* revealed. For example, Saul of Tarsus.

He saw 'a light from heaven, above the brightness of the sun'. This left him blind. Out of the heaven of heavens, through the heavens, lighting the chosen man on the earth, came the uttermost beams from the presence of the uncreated Light.

Saul could not see so far as to the roof of heaven: even in what he could see, he could not bear the sun in its brightness. Here was a light, however, *the true Light*, the exceeding radiant beams of which pierced three heavens, and withal blinded the man on the Damascus road.

And yet these beams could not in any wise remotely indicate the unbearable intensity of that source from whence they came. Out of *that* very source, however, came the words, rolling down the steeps of the heavens, 'I am Jesus'.

So that when Moses wrote by the Holy Ghost, Genesis 1:1, 'In the beginning God created the heaven and the earth', and again, 'Let there be light', Genesis 1:3, the meaning is that God had first *wrought* by his power—or, colloquially speaking, first *made* with his *hands*—but then *entered* in his *presence*. 'And there was light.'

The ensuing dividing of the light from the darkness, called respectively Day and Night, does not and cannot mean day and night proceeding *from the same source as that brought in on the fourth day*, Genesis 1:14-19. It means that *before* the sun was made, its effect was anticipated by him who purposed to create it, so that *substantially* the same thing—though infinitely greater in intensity—already existed.

Where his real presence subsisted, *there* was the light. Where not, it was darkness. That darkness and light, day and night, alternated *before* the bringing in of the sun, with its rising and setting, shows that 'known unto God are all his works from the beginning of the world', Acts 15:18.

It also reveals that for three days God bore witness from the foundation of the world to the end of time that — over and above man not living by bread alone—humanity must never assume vision to be adequate, if all that can be seen is that which is illuminated by mere outward light.

'And God said, Let there be a firmament in the midst of the waters, and let it divide the waters from the waters. And God made'—the Hebrew is *Asah*, to make; as opposed to *Bara*, to create—'God made the firmament, and divided the waters which were under the firmament from the waters which were above the firmament: and it was so.

'And God called the firmament Heaven. And the evening and the morning were the second day', Genesis 1:6-8.

As on each day, God wrought through the night to bring his work to light in the morning. In this case, he divided the waters so as to form a vast expanse or firmament. This is the second case of division. The first was that of the light from the darkness. This is that of the waters under the firmament from the waters above the firmament.

No attempt whatsoever is made to satisfy the intellectual pretensions of man. Enough is said to satisfy the meek. The word of God is for faith. There is no provision of information or for education to divert the mind whilst fallen mankind hurtles on his way to the abyss of everlasting perdition, through the inferno of a melting universe.

What has been revealed is enough. God does not go beyond because of the ever-present danger of diversion through the unrestrained and useless intellectual curiosity of a world condemned already. In such a case nothing matters but the knowledge of salvation.

Further to understanding Genesis 1:1 to 2:3, two things ought to be grasped. First, the 'old world', destroyed beyond recognition by the Flood, was not as the present world.

So interprets Peter: 'By the word of God the heavens were of old, and the earth standing out of the water and in the water.' This precisely describes what is recorded in Genesis 1:6-8. Peter continues, especially concerning the water, '*Whereby* the world that then was, being overflowed with water, perished', II Peter 3:5,6.

Secondly, it is necessary to make the point that until the last five hundred years it was generally supposed that the earth was flat, and, indeed, until comparatively recent times this misconception was not uncommon.

Yet—however laughable this may appear to be at first—to all practical purposes *in experience* the earth seems to be flat. That it is not *really* so makes no essential difference to most ordinary individuals.

Hence the word of God does not attempt to enlighten men on such things. The Creator knew what he had created. Such as Kepler, Copernicus, and Galileo found out a fraction of what he had created.

It may well be that men were better off knowing less, rather than glorying over the infinitely tiny sum of information which

53

now convinces them that they know everything; that no one knew anything worthwhile before them; and that the Creator—if he existed—knew so little about anything that he may as well be considered superfluous.

Yet it was out of love to man that God limited the extent of human knowledge of natural phenomena, so that humanity might stay within the bounds of safety. In hatred to man Satan drew humanity past those bounds, creating an insatiable curiosity, whilst ensuring an everlasting destruction.

Of course now I will be regaled with the wonders of science. What wonders? Chernobyl? The threat of destruction to the species? The overturning of the ecology? Genetic engineering? The letting loose of forces within and without mankind that have long past escaped control? The impossibility of averting an unthinkable series of impending global disasters?

What wonders? Misery, pain, grief, and anguish are greater, not less. Disease, corruption, maiming, and death exact precisely the same—if not an even greater—toll as they did aeons ago, when man first embarked on this insane folly that now threatens all living existence.

Said the wise man, 'The heart of the sons of men is full of evil, and madness is in their heart while they live, and after that they go to the dead', Ecclesiastes 9:3.

I say, man *naturally* supposes the earth to be a flat surface, and the limitation of this knowledge is practically less damaging—on the vast scale of things—than the possession of scientific information beyond the capacity of mankind to control. In any event, flat or round, God made no effort to inform man otherwise.

Psalm 136:6 speaks of God stretching out the earth above the waters. The word of God condescends to the capacity of man's understanding of the earth, whilst carefully instructing him in the knowledge of God. The wise of this world think to do it the other way round.

Isa. 11:12 speaks of the four corners of the earth. Ezekiel 7:2 declares, 'An end, the end is come upon the four corners of the land.' Though everybody knows that *literally* the land of Israel had not four corners.

Peter, whilst praying, saw in a trance a vision 'As it had been a great sheet, let down from heaven by four corners', Acts 10:11; 11:5. This indicated the gospel going out to the Gentile nations, even to the four corners of the earth. And so it came to pass.

Just so Genesis 1:6-8—and, indeed, Genesis 1:1 to 2:3—is written to accommodate the condition of understanding that then existed—and was to exist, in the huge range of time, until *comparatively* recent times—in the mind of man.

To grasp what is being *revealed*—as opposed to the bare facts from which that revelation takes its rise—one must think of the earth in terms of a *flat surface*, just as most modern men accept it in actual practice despite their theoretic knowledge.

It is *that* which was depicted as being without form and void. With the heaven vastly above, and the abyss profoundly below, and the dark waters rolling across. *That best describes the indescribable* in God's great kindness to man over what in any event lies beyond his capacity of comprehension, namely, the Creation.

When the conclusion of the first day brought the work of God to light, then the firmament was made, transforming *that* situation.

The firmament, or expanse, was raised over the watery surface of the earth, so that now a great space, called Heaven, stood between the waters above the earth, and the waters which constituted the surface of the earth. Below that surface was the watery abyss.

'And there was evening and there was morning: second day.' So the Hebrew reads. But whilst on the first day 'God saw the light, that it was good', and, moreover, good is pronounced on every other day, not on this. As if the overhanging waters, and the great deep, were appointed—laid up in store—against the judgment of the great Flood in the day of wrath, according to the foreknowledge of God.

On the evening and the morning of the third day, what came to light was that the waters — swirling over the surface of the earth under the heaven—by the word of God had been gathered together unto one place. The dry land had appeared. God called the dry land Earth; and the gathering together of the waters called he Seas. And God saw that it was good.

And God commanded the earth to bring forth grass, the herb yielding seed, and the fruit tree yielding fruit after his kind, whose seed is in itself, upon the earth. And it was so. And God saw that it was good.

And what a day was this! It was the third day. It was the first day of the creation of living things, of self-propagating life. God created it, and he did so from nothing, commanding the earth itself that it should bring forth this living, verdant mantle.

'And God said, Let there be lights in the firmament of the heaven to divide the day from the night; and let them be for signs, and for seasons, and for days, and years', Genesis 1:14. These lights must never be confused with the true Light of the first day. They are nothing in comparison.

Moreover, although the clock of time began to tick, and the pendulum of the age to swing, on this the fourth day, it was still the *fourth* day.

This was so that men might learn their nothingness. For by nothing save the power of God, in a divine mystery, *three days previously* both light and darkness, day and night, anticipated the day of the beaming of the sun and the light of the moon upon the shining seas and verdant earth.

How marvellous to consider that, carried through the waters of the Flood, from thence — that is, God's work on the third day — springs every blade of grass upon which we look; every shrub that we behold; and every tree that we see growing upon the face of the earth!

God created all, causing the earth to bring forth overnight where hitherto there had been nothing: no, not so much as dry land even the day before. But from henceforth, the seed of each kind being within itself, everything should be—and has been—propagated by its own seed until this day.

Upon this vista the sun has risen day by day, from the fourth day until now. Over it night has fallen and the moon waxed and waned consistently, to this latest hour. And this at the command of him who divided the light from the darkness, and ordained the sun and the moon to shed light upon his own work. How marvellous are thy works, O God, and that my soul knoweth right well.

The following two days are the days in which higher forms of life were created, not now to clothe the earth with vegetation, but that the waters and the earth might bring forth moving and living creatures, each after his kind, and all blessed and commanded to multiply. All these were destined to be brought under the dominion of man, the crowning work of the Creator.

On the fifth day, between the evening and the morning—so that all came to light with the rising beams of the sun in the heavens—God commanded the waters to bring forth abundantly the moving creature that hath life, and fowl that may fly above the earth in the open firmament of heaven.

'And God created great whales, and every living creature that moveth, which the waters brought forth abundantly, after their kind, and every winged fowl after his kind: and God saw that it was good.

'And God blessed them, saying, Be fruitful, and multiply, and fill the waters in the seas, and let fowl multiply in the earth. And the evening and the morning were the fifth day', Genesis 1:20-23. All were created in a day, and each was created after his kind on that same day. The day before none existed. That day all had come into existence.

Thereafter every sort—after its kind—was to reproduce itself: 'Be fruitful, and multiply.' Then, not a fish that one beholds, neither a bird of the air that one sees, but by subsequent natural generation all sprang from this unique Creation of God.

Just as on the fifth day the waters were commanded to bring forth abundantly the moving creature that hath life, and fowl that may fly, so between the evening and the morning of the sixth day the earth was caused likewise to bear in abundance.

'And God said, Let the earth bring forth the living creature after his kind, and cattle after their kind, and everything that creepeth upon the earth after his kind: and God saw that it was good', Genesis 1:24,25.

Now, on this same day, there follows the apex of Creation: 'And God said, Let us make man in our image, after our likeness', Genesis 1:26. Man was to have dominion over all Creation. 'The heaven, even the heavens, are the LORD's: but the earth hath he given to the children of men', Psalm 115:16.

'So God created'—it is *Bara*, create; as opposed to *Asah*, make: one can *make* from what was *there*; but *creation* is from *nothing*— 'So God created man in his own image, in the image of God created he him; male and female created he them', Genesis 1:27.

Of this, and of the comparison between the creation of man recorded in Genesis 1:1 to 2:3, in which the name ELOHIM appears thirty-three times, and appears exclusively; as opposed to the second account, from Genesis 2:4, in which the name JEHOVAH is *added* to that of ELOHIM, I shall have more to say at a later time. Suffice it to observe here, 'God created man in his own image', Gen. 1:27.

What image is that? The context should determine the mind of the Spirit as to the interpretation in this place. One should enquire, What has been seen, and what is to be seen, of the image and likeness of God in this context, Genesis 1:1 to 2:3?

First, God is light. Since he divided the light from the darkness, and this division is repeated as an ordinance of the heavens for the instruction of man, it is proper to conclude from this place with John, 'God is light, and in him *is no darkness at all.*' That is the image of God in man.

Second, God delights in life. His word causes life to spring up into being from the dry land, so that grass, herbs, trees, and all manner of verdure clothe the earth with living beauty.

The waters are commanded to bring forth *abundantly* the moving creature that hath life, and the fowls that may fly above the earth in the open firmament of heaven. Life teems in the waters, and the flocks gathering everywhere above testify of God's love of life.

Finally the earth, first commanded to bring forth grass, herb, and trees, now brings forth the living creature after his kind, the beast of the earth, cattle, and everything that creepeth upon the earth. Every element, the whole sphere, is filled with living things from the heights in the heaven to the depths of the earth. Heaven and earth are filled with life, and life more abundant.

The very Creation, at first without form and void, is now orderly and purposeful, with a diversity of life that must of necessity reflect *the delight of the Creator*. But that life which is in his image and likeness was reserved for the creation of man. Man in God's image reflects divine life and vigour.

Death has no place in this. 'The dead praise not the LORD, neither any that go down into silence', Psalm 115:17. In Israel, contact with death brought exclusion from God: 'Whosoever toucheth the dead body of any man that is dead, and purifieth not himself, defileth the tabernacle of the LORD; and that soul shall be cut off from Israel', Numbers 19:13. Death has no place in the image and likeness of God.

Again, before Creation existed, from everlasting God is. If so, as saith the apostle John, God is a *Spirit*, Jn. 4:24. Then, above all, the image and likeness of God in man must reflect *spirituality*, just as every quality and characteristic of true humanity—in the image and likeness of God—must be spiritual.

Observe that no creature fed on another: following the creation of man, and his blessing, with the divine expression of God's delight that man's life should be multiplied abundantly in procreation, and that he should have dominion over all, the question of food arises, Genesis 1:29,30.

The food of man was to be the herb bearing seed, and the fruit of the trees. Now, this may be plucked and eaten without destruction either to plant or tree.

The food of the beasts, fowls, and creeping things likewise was provided by every green herb. These herbs, however devoured, yielded nourishment to the eater without dying in the process. There was *no* death. The trees, the herbs, the grass, replenished themselves and were preserved in life. Life before God is of the essence that man—and his dominion—should bear his image and likeness.

It would perhaps be too much to say that this context — Genesis 1:1 to 2:3 — reveals that God is love, although undoubtedly that is at the heart of his image and likeness, I John 4:8,16. Withal too much to say, yet, perhaps, not too much to observe that in context there appears some slight indication, some faint spiritual allusion to the love of God in one place and another.

There are the *things* that he loves: order; beauty; arrangement; development to perfection. He loves life. He loves goodness. Seven times over to perfection he beheld, he saw, it pleased him to look and behold 'that it was good'. Very good. This cannot spring but from love.

His care for what he had created and made: 'his tender mercies are over all his works', Psalm 145:9. His care in his provision for every living thing, so that no life, however lowly, should be damaged. His care for, and delight in, the man that should bear his likeness and his image. If this does not hint at love, What does?

Finally, his rest. 'Thus the heavens and the earth were finished, and all the host of them. And on the seventh day God ended his work which he had made; and he rested on the seventh day from all his work which he had made.

'And God blessed the seventh day, and sanctified it: because that in it he had rested from all his work which God created and made', Genesis 2:1-3.

He rests in his love. Nothing less could bring such contentment. His rest, his being at peace, his satisfaction, must be indicative of his loving the perfection of that Creation — crowned with the image and likeness of God in man—brought to fulfilment.

But how could that be, if love were not his nature, and, above all, love for man its expression? Then, love, the love of God, must be his likeness and image in man.

But what man? I answer, That man foreshadowed in the ELOHIM passage, in which truths are included or excluded from the creation of Adam, so that there should appear no mere recorded account but 'the figure of him that was to come'. Then its element must be prophetic.

Prophetic? Of Creation? But what Creation? Not this Creation, which is destined for that last day in which 'the heavens shall pass away with a great noise, and the elements shall melt with fervent heat, the earth also and the works that are therein shall be burned up', II Peter 3:10.

Nevertheless, retaining and omitting details from the entire factual account of this Creation, the ELOHIM passage, Genesis 1:1 to 2:3, points — but so faintly — to the world to come, whereof we speak.

God rested? That day, yes. But thereafter? After the Fall? 'My Father worketh hitherto, and I work.' God did not, and God could not, rest in a scene of cursing, sin, and death, a scene brought in by the Fall of the first man and the curse upon the first Creation.

But, in his very nature, despite the Fall and the curse, God purposed righteousness and life, salvation and redemption, in Another Man and for Another Creation. Now, as Genesis 1:1 to 2:3 foreshadow, in *that* Man, and in *that* Creation, he *will* rest. So will his people. 'For we which have believed do enter into rest', Heb. 4:3.

Although God's works were finished from the foundation of the world, still, since the Fall of that world, he had no more rest in it than had his people. Yet he spake in a certain place of the seventh day on this wise, And God did rest the seventh day from all his works.

That was *that* seventh day, Genesis 2:2,3. Then the Fall. Aeons later, the Holy Ghost spake of sabbath-keeping Israel

'*If* they shall enter into my rest.' And again, 'I sware in my wrath, They'—sabbath-keeping Israel—'shall *not* enter into my rest.' But they supposed that they *had* rested *with him* when they rested on the sabbath.

But he was not resting. He was working. He was working for another Man, another Creation, and a rest everlasting, all yet to come.

As to that, said he of those unbelieving apostates, 'They shall *not* enter into my rest.' Not *that* rest. For to all those who rest in the first Adam and the first Creation, for all their religion, 'I sware *in my wrath*, They shall *not* enter into my rest'.

That is, his future rest. His rest in the *last* Adam. In the *second* man. In the resurrection from the dead. In the *new* Creation. In the everlasting *inheritance*. Whence it follows, Heb. 4:9, 'There remaineth therefore a rest to the people of God.' Amen.

III

Creation: The JEHOVAH Elohim Account

IN the opening chapters of Genesis what immediately strikes the eye is the way in which the record of the Creation is *repeated*.

There is not just *one* account. There are *two* accounts of Creation. These differ in length, content, and emphasis. This in itself indicates a profound mystery. Yet a mystery rarely noticed, seldom considered, and hardly opened.

The first account of the Creation begins at Genesis 1:1 and ends at 2:3. These verses are characterized by the name ELOHIM —translated GOD in the English bible—used exclusively in this passage and occurring thirty-three times.

The remainder of chapter two — that is, verses 4 to 25 — presents the second record of the Creation. This is worded in a completely different manner and considered from an entirely distinct aspect. Throughout this passage the divine name Elohim is marked by the addition of the name JEHOVAH, so as to read JEHOVAH Elohim, translated LORD God in the English bible. This name occurs eleven times in these verses.

I cannot repeat sufficiently that the opening chapters of Genesis are written to convey hidden mysteries. Far from giving what would be termed a 'scientific' series of data concerning Creation—although stating categorical facts as the basis—the reason for writing is *spiritual*. It is so that *spiritual* things should thus be conveyed. And, if so, in a mystery.

64

He that does not come to Genesis, to the Creation, with the profound reverence which such a realization genders, might just as well not come at all. Such a person will understand nothing, and nothing will be conveyed to him. As saith the scripture, 'Now we have received, not the spirit of the world, but the spirit which is of God; that we might know the things that are freely given to us of God.'

For 'the things of God knoweth no man, but the Spirit of God.' 'Which things also we speak, not in the words which man's wisdom teacheth, but which the Holy Ghost teacheth; comparing spiritual things with spiritual.'

In the first account of Creation, Genesis 1:1 to 2:3, in which the divine name ELOHIM—and no other—occurs thirty-three times, the seven consecutive days of Creation are recorded. Man is created in the image and likeness of God, and 'male and female created he them', as destined for dominion over all the earth. The divine name ELOHIM is absolute and inscrutable. Nothing is revealed save the work which he did.

This is not so with the name JEHOVAH Elohim. JEHOVAH is the name by which God made himself known to Israel under the law given by Moses, whose first book is that of Genesis. JEHOVAH was not revealed to any other nation. 'He showeth his word unto Jacob, his statutes and his judgments unto Israel.'

We are indebted to Israel for the first book of Moses: Genesis was written *for Israel*. 'He hath not dealt so with any nation: and as for his judgments, they have not known them. Praise ye JEHOVAH', Psalm 147:19,20.

In this second—JEHOVAH Elohim—account there is little of the detail found in the first. Nothing is said of the seven days. Only a line or two records the Creation itself. Much is taken for granted from Genesis 1:1 to 2:3. But in the second account a great deal is added, particularly of events *personal to Adam*.

Indeed, the name Adam is not mentioned in the first account; neither is the ground—*Adamah* in the Hebrew—nor the fact that Adam was to be a living soul. Eden is not mentioned. Neither is the tree of life, nor the tree of the knowledge of good and evil.

Whoever can put a difference between the two accounts, observing what is peculiar to each, discerning the reason for the distinction, that man is in the secret, and understands the mystery.

The second — JEHOVAH Elohim — account concerns *Adam*, introducing him *by name*. Indeed the record *centres* on Adam, focusing on his manhood, his history, and his posterity. All this, seeing that he is the head of the fallen race, makes the second account of immense importance to mankind, without the knowledge of which every man and all nations must grope for the wall like the blind under thick darkness.

JEHOVAH was that covenant name by which God enjoined the children of Israel unto himself. The seed of Abraham, Isaac, and Jacob, Israel was chosen out from all nations to be his— JEHOVAH'S—peculiar covenant people.

Now, Moses enunciated the covenant—for the law was given by Moses—and, having spoken every precept to all the people according to the law, took the blood of calves and of goats, with water, and scarlet wool, and hyssop, and sprinkled *both the book*, and all the people.

But of the five volumes written by Moses constituting that book—called the *Torah*—the first volume, Genesis, was given to Israel so that the people—the chosen people of JEHOVAH— might go back beyond Abraham, Isaac, and Jacob, and find their ultimate origin and root in Adam under the divine name JEHOVAH Elohim.

'These are the generations'—writes Moses to Israel—'of the heavens and of the earth when they were created, in the day that JEHOVAH Elohim made the earth and the heavens', Genesis 2:4. This shows the beginning of the revelation of JEHOVAH to Israel, made known in Adam.

Observe the interchangeability of terms in this verse: first 'the heavens and the earth'; then, 'the earth and the heavens'.

God's thoughts were for the harmony of heaven and earth, not for their disruption. It was not his mind that he should be in the heavens aloof from the earth, and that men should be on earth detached from the heavens. His mind, expressly, was that heaven and earth should be in harmony; that earth and heaven should be united.

'The heavens and the earth.' 'The earth and the heavens', Genesis 2:4. Here is as it were a ladder set up on the earth, with its top reaching even to heaven. In this vision, to be revealed later in Genesis, JEHOVAH was at the head of the ladder, and Jacob—soon to be named Israel—was at the foot, with the angels of God ascending and descending upon it.

In such a case—heavens, earth; earth, heavens—'Truth shall spring out of the earth; and righteousness shall look down from heaven. Yea, JEHOVAH shall give that which is good; and our land shall yield her increase', Psalm 85:11,12. Such a prospect is in view, even as Moses by the Holy Ghost indicates the harmony of heaven and earth, earth and heaven, Genesis 2:4.

After the words 'JEHOVAH Elohim made the earth and the heavens,'—note the comma—the fifth verse continues 'And every plant of the field before it was in the earth, and every herb of the field before it grew.'

The ambiguity of this wording is obvious. 'Before *it*'? Before *what*? Before JEHOVAH Elohim made the earth and the heavens? How could that be?

The translation is correct in itself: the *arrangement of the words is not*, resulting in an impossible situation. By following the arrangement of the Septuagint too slavishly, the translators have set the correct words in the wrong place, resulting in an unintelligible contradiction.

As verse 5 stands—again notice the comma at the end of verse 4—JEHOVAH Elohim, who made the earth and the heavens, also made every plant *before it was in the earth.* Likewise the wording implies that he made the herbs *even before they existed.*

As literally as I can render, the Hebrew actually reads, 'And every bush of the field not yet was it in the earth; and every green herb of the field not yet was it sprung up.' Here I must confess the Revised Version to have given a more accurate sense: 'And no plant of the field was yet in the earth, and no herb of the field had yet sprung up.'

Not that I would ever recommend that thin end of the wedge the Revised Version—much less its increasingly corrupt successors—under any circumstances.

By far the safest course must be to stick with the Authorized, because of its overwhelming *overall* accuracy, and—covering so long a time—its divinely attested Greek edition.

However, in the comparatively rare instances of the translators' ineptitude—such as Genesis 2:5—one should rearrange in one's mind the order of the words so that the passage makes sense.

Thus one would adjust the verse, First, by bringing the word 'before' to the front of the clause, and, next, by dropping the word 'it' altogether.

The verse now reads 'And *before* any plant of the field was in the earth, and *before* every herb of the field grew.' This answers to the translation virtually word for word, save for dropping the superfluous 'it'. But such a rearrangement makes all the difference.

It is obvious that this gives the sense. Observe the wording of verse 4 once again: 'These are the generations of the heavens and of the earth when they were created, *in the day* that JEHOVAH Elohim made the earth and the heavens,'.

Now, *that* day was the *first* day, Genesis 1:1. But—again note the translators' comma at the end of 2:4—Genesis 2:5 *continues* to speak of the condition of things—described in Genesis 1:2 as being without form and void—*on that same day.*

That is, the *first* day, three days *before* any plant was in the earth, and *before* any herb of the field grew. It was the first day of Creation, Genesis 1:1-5. Of this day, Genesis 2:4,5 speaks. Not until the *third* day—Genesis 1:9-13—did vegetation appear on the earth.

To summarize: the words 'in the day' — Genesis 2:4,5 — correspond with *the first day* of Genesis 1:1-5.

Genesis 2:5, immediately following the comma at the close of the previous verse, informs the reader that *the day of Creation* was *before* any vegetation existed. But this is put in such a way that *from the very first day*, the verdure to come on the third day was anticipated: indeed, the anticipation of it was essential to the JEHOVAH Elohim context.

Why essential to the context? Because it is a context concerning *Adam*, and *the work* of Adam. For as the juxtaposition of 'the heavens and the earth' and 'the earth and the heavens' indicates a harmony, so that harmony requires the presence of *man* upon the earth, and man *cultivating* the earth in order to fulfil the will of JEHOVAH Elohim.

Hence the verse continues—concerning the day, the *first* day, of the Creation, the earth being without form and void—'*Before* every plant of the field was in the earth, and *before* every herb of the field grew: *for JEHOVAH Elohim had not caused it to rain upon the earth, and there was not a man to till the ground.*'

In a word, it was the mind of JEHOVAH Elohim in Creation that, the heavens and the earth—the earth and the heavens—being in harmony, the ground should become clothed with verdure, with every plant and every herb of the field in abundance, *so that man, that is, Adam, should till the ground that it might bring forth more abundantly.* For this the Creation was formed, and this the first day anticipated.

The conclusion of verse 5, 'for JEHOVAH Elohim had not caused it to rain upon the earth, and there was not a man to till the ground', seems mystifying. It is as though the *reason* neither plant nor herb was in the earth was because of the lack of rain and the absence of man.

In fact the earth was clothed with verdure on the third day, Genesis 1:9-13, whereas man was not created until the sixth day, Genesis 1:24-31. And as to rain, this did not fall until the Flood. So how could the lack of rain and the absence of man be the reason for there being no verdure?

Because of the difference in the viewpoint of the narrative. Chapter 1:1 to 2:3 states the events that took place in seven days, and the view of man on the sixth day *uses the narrative of those events* so as to point to and foreshadow a Man and a Creation yet to come.

Not so chapter 2:4,5. Creation is briefly mentioned, but here the first man Adam is *the* subject of the narrative. The Creation awaited *his* being formed, to reach the fulfilment of its purpose. Israel, chosen of JEHOVAH, should consider his origins, and ponder that purpose.

For the first book of Moses—and particularly the JEHOVAH Elohim passage—was written to a covenant people, an *agricultural* people. But Moses wrote Genesis long, long after the events of Creation. Then, such a people, to whom agriculture was life itself, knew well by bitter experience that without rain everything ended in drought and death.

To Israel, rain was essential for cultivation. Then, to such a people, rain would have appeared to be essential for the man who was their progenitor, the object of Creation to JEHOVAH. Rain was the *blessing* upon the land of Israel. The people could not conceive of the earth without rain. Then where was it in Genesis 2:4,5?

It was not in Genesis 2:4,5 at all. 'But there went up a mist from the earth, and watered the whole face of the ground', Genesis 2:6. Note that this reference to the mist is omitted from Genesis 1:9-13. The omission is because Adam's cultivation of the ground—*Adamah*—was not at all in view in this earlier—ELOHIM—account.

Formerly the moisturizing mist was not mentioned; latterly it was essential that it should be mentioned, sustaining and nourishing the growth of every plant, and every herb of the field, with a view to cultivation.

Hence, observing the absence of both plant and herb in the day of Creation, Moses informs Israel—accustomed to total dependence upon JEHOVAH for rain—that JEHOVAH Elohim had not caused it to rain upon the earth, neither was there a man to till the ground, Genesis 2:5. Immediately, however, he adds, but there *was* mist, and there *came* man, Genesis 2:6. And for what purpose? 'To till the ground.'

The mist, by which the whole face of the ground was watered from—at least—the third day until the Deluge, provided the source from which the grass, every plant of the field, every herb thereof, and every tree, was given moisture, sustaining the growth of the verdant Creation. In a peculiar sense this pertained to Adam. It was before the Fall and until the Deluge.

This mist pertained to *Adam* tilling the ground. It was for him—and, in due time, his posterity—to cultivate the earth. Hence in the second—JEHOVAH Elohim—account, not only is the name Adam introduced, but also *Adamah*, the ground. Likewise 'field': an area of cultivation. The same thing applies to 'tillage': Adam was to 'till' the ground.

The word 'plant' is introduced in the second account: so is 'mist'; 'form' — Adam was 'formed' — and 'dust'. These are things *belonging* to Adam, and spoken expressly to Israel by JEHOVAH Elohim.

Adam was of the earth, earthy. So says the apostle Paul, I Cor. 15:47, 'The first man is of the earth, earthy'. His work— and that of his posterity, was the tillage of the ground: to bring forth fruit from this world. This worldliness obtains still after the Fall, when it appears, 'As is the earthy, such are they also that are earthy', I Cor. 15:48.

The next but one occurrence of the Hebrew word translated 'till' comes after Adam's fall: 'Therefore JEHOVAH Elohim sent him forth from the garden of Eden, to *till* the ground from whence he was taken. So he drove out the man', Genesis 3:23,24.

Likewise an ominous succession appears in Adam's progeny Cain, who slew his brother Abel. Of this murderer it is written, and not without purpose, Genesis 4:2, '*But* Cain was a tiller of the ground.' Cain bore the image and likeness of fallen Adam, not that of God.

And can such a man as Adam, even before the Fall, in or of himself be the man envisaged in Genesis 1:1 to 2:3? Literally— of course—the creation of the first man Adam was the occasion of the record of Genesis 1:26,27.

But that so much is omitted peculiar to Adam, and that so much is retained figurative of Christ, points to the inevitable conclusion that the ELOHIM account provides a figure of him that was to come. Selecting what is to purpose from the first man, and the present Creation, the Holy Ghost by Moses foreshadows the second Man, and promises a new Creation.

'And so it is written, The first man Adam was made a living soul; the last Adam was made a quickening spirit. Howbeit that was not first which is spiritual, but that which is natural: and afterward that which is spiritual. The first man is of the earth, earthy: the second man is the Lord from heaven', I Cor. 15:45-48.

But from the beginning of the world, from the creation of the natural man, from the record of Creation, and the truth of the forming of earthy man, the Holy Ghost draws out that which is applicable to envisage the heavenly Man who was yet to come, setting this foreshadowing by itself apart. This appears in Genesis 1:1 to 2:3. What appears? A shadow of Christ, and a foretaste of the world to come.

Therefore consider the creation of man from Genesis 1:26-28, the first account, 'And ELOHIM said, Let us make man in our image, after our likeness: and let them' — that is, male and female—'have dominion over the fish of the sea, and over the fowl of the air, and over the cattle, and over all the earth, and over every creeping thing that creepeth upon the earth.

'So ELOHIM created man in his own image, in the image of God created he him; male and female created he them.

'And ELOHIM blessed them, and ELOHIM said unto them, Be fruitful, and multiply, and replenish the earth, and subdue it: and have dominion over the fish of the sea, and over the fowl of the air, and over every living thing that moveth upon the earth.'

73

Written strictly and literally of Adam, yet vital matter is left out of this ELOHIM record which is so distinctive of that first man: for example, his very name Adam; the name of the dust of the ground—*Adamah*—from which he was formed; his being a living soul; and, besides this, much other detail is deliberately omitted.

Nevertheless unique things are *retained*—in this first, ELOHIM, account — concerning the creation of man *which aptly and unquestionably frame the passage so that it becomes prophetic of Christ, the second Man, the last Adam, the One in whom all living should trust.*

This is not to say that nothing at all in the subsequent JEHOVAH Elohim account is prophetic of Christ. For example, in the forming—the Hebrew is 'building'—of the woman from the bone and flesh of Adam, and the exclamation of Adam when he awoke to see what JEHOVAH Elohim had wrought, Genesis 2:21-24.

From this very place the apostle Paul quotes the remarkable words of Adam, and applies them mystically to Christ and his bride, see Ephesians 5:30-32.

This shows that in the eternal purpose of God—even before the Fall—Adam himself in innocence was to look for and hope in Another yet to come, of whom he himself was but the figure, and therefore in whom he should put all his confidence. Then why should it come as any surprise to see Christ foreshadowed so early as Genesis 1:26-28?

The main emphasis in Genesis 1:26-28 lies in the concept of 'image and likeness', together with that of 'dominion'.

It has been indicated that what the ELOHIM passage discloses of the divine image and likeness—eternal, almighty, inscrutable —is that of light; life; spirit; and, it may be, love. But—as to that image—whatever may have been true of Adam in innocence, of necessity this was but the palest reflection of the brightness of God's glory manifest in Christ in the fulness of time.

That *two* men, one of earthy creation, the other of eternal purpose, were determined in the counsels of God before the Creation of the world, and manifest—one in substance, the other in shadow—from the foundation of it, is evident. Hence the conclusion of the apostle Paul, 'As we have borne the image of the earthy, we shall also bear the image of the heavenly', I Cor. 15:49.

But the earthy *was* earthy, by definition, *before* the Fall. And if the pale reflection of the image and likeness of ELOHIM was borne in an earthen vessel, What of that? As to the divine image and likeness in the heavenly, this is another thing. *Being* heavenly, he is the Son. Then, he is the image of his Father. But that is very, very far from—it transcends beyond measure—the image and likeness of ELOHIM in Adam.

This image of the Father in Christ, revealed in the gospel of God concerning his Son, is glimpsed in the promise of that gospel from the foundation of the world. Now, however, the Son is risen, and 'God, who commanded the light to shine out of darkness, hath shined in our hearts, to give the light of the knowledge of the glory of God *in the face of Jesus Christ*', II Cor. 4:6.

What if some do not believe? What if some have not believed from the foundation of the world? What if some did not believe the Son at his coming?

Paul answers every question, 'But if our gospel be hid, it is hid to them that are lost: in whom the god of this world hath blinded the minds of them which believe not, lest the light of the glorious gospel of Christ, who *is* the image of God, should shine unto them', II Cor. 4:3,4.

75

Here is no reflected image in a vessel of clay. Here is the very essence of the thing in a body of glory. If so, in another Man, a second Man, a last Adam, 'Who *is* the *image* of the invisible God', Col. 1:15.

And to conclude the matter, it was not said—it could not be said—of Adam; but it was said—it must be said—of the Son of the Father: 'Being the *brightness* of his glory, and the *express* image of his person', Heb. 1:3.

Next, Adam was to have dominion over the fish of the sea, and over the fowl of the air, and over the cattle, and over all the earth, and over every creeping thing that creepeth upon the earth, so as to be fruitful, and multiply, and replenish the earth, and subdue it. *But this never happened.*

Adam in innocence never brought this blessing to the earth. Adam in the Fall brought the curse to the earth, till by it, through his posterity, the earth was filled with blood.

Then shall their unbelief make the faith of God of none effect? God forbid. For now *another* Man appears, and *another* world is in view, by whom and in which every promise of hope shall be fulfilled.

Hence the psalmist queries, What is man that thou art mindful of him? and the son of man that thou visitest him? The answer of God is, not the first, but the second Man. Not corrupt man, but the Son of man. Not a fallen Adam, but a risen Christ.

Having asked the rhetorical question, What is man? the psalmist is moved by the Holy Ghost to answer. 'Thou hast made him a little lower than the angels, and hast crowned him with glory and honour. Thou madest him to have dominion over the works of thy hands; thou hast put all things under his feet:

'All sheep and oxen, yea, and the beasts of the field; the fowl of the air, and the fish of the sea, and whatsoever passeth through the paths of the seas', Psalm 8:4-8. But of whom, and of whose dominion, does the psalmist speak? Not of fallen Adam, but of the ascended Son. Not of the first man in his ignominy, but the second Man in his glory. And this is easily proved.

The author of the epistle to the Hebrews bears witness by the Holy Ghost to the Son, observing, 'But one in a certain place testified, saying, What is man, that thou art mindful of him?'—this quotation being from Psalm 8, it follows that this psalm is the certain place quoted, and the psalmist is the one who testified—'or the son of man, that thou visitest him?

'Thou madest him a little lower than the angels; thou crownedst him with glory and honour, and didst set him over the works of thy hands: Thou hast put all things in subjection under his feet', Hebrews 2:6-8.

The new testament epistle quotes the ancient psalm. But to whom is the writer of the Hebrews applying that psalm? Observe, 'For in that he put all in subjection under him'—under whom? Why, under man; under the son of man: but the question is, Which man? Adam or Christ?—'in that he put all in subjection under him, he left nothing that is not put under him.'

The writer goes on, 'But now we see not yet all things put under him.' Under whom? Why, under the feet of the *same man of whom the psalmist wrote.* But, I repeat, which man is that? Hebrews continues immediately, having stated that we see *not yet* all things put under him, 'But we see Jesus'—then, *that* is the man whom the psalmist had in view, and of whom the writer of the epistle to the Hebrews testified.

'But we see *Jesus,* who was made a little lower than the angels for the suffering of death, crowned with glory and honour', Hebrews 2:8,9. Now Adam was never crowned with glory and honour. Then this cannot be written of Adam. But we see Jesus crowned with glory and honour. Then this must be testified of him.

If so, since the dominion and subjection of all things in Genesis 1:26-28 ostensibly appears to be spoken of and to the *first* man, then, because *the words only apply*—and are *in fact applied* in the epistle to the Hebrews—to the *second* Man, it follows that this passage in the first book of Moses speaks of Christ, as he said, 'Moses wrote of me'.

Notwithstanding that the writer of the epistle to the Hebrews applies Genesis 1:26-28 to *Christ*, one might object that the words were spoken originally to *Adam*. But not without qualification in a mystery, for this is the ELOHIM passage, in which it has been shown *that Adam's name is deliberately omitted*, and not only so, but, in figure, type, and shadow, Christ's name is writ large over all the page.

But, if it be of Christ, what of that Creation? As it was with Adam, so it was with that Creation. It has been shown that the first man in Genesis 1:26-28 prefigures the second; and so it follows from the same place—as taught in Psalm 8—that the first Creation, the world that then was, foreshadowed that which is to come.

Of this the apostle, writing in the epistle to the Hebrews, bears witness. For *immediately preceding* Heb. 2:6-8—the passage quoting the eighth psalm — he wrote 'For unto the angels hath he not put in subjection *the world to come*, whereof we speak', Heb. 2:5.

Then, Hebrews speaks, Psalm 8 quotes, and Genesis 1 foreshadows not *this* world, but *that*, to which the writer of the Hebrews refers, saying, 'Of which we speak'. 'We' being Moses; the psalmist; and the apostles. But of *what* world did they speak? Why, of the world *to come*, not of this world, as he says, 'The world to come, whereof we speak', Heb. 2:5.

In contrast, however, we read of another world, not to come, but now present, the world that now is, of which Moses bare record in the volume of the book; and of another man, the first man Adam, of whom JEHOVAH Elohim spake to Israel.

Writing to the children of Israel Moses records, 'And JEHOVAH Elohim formed man of the dust of the ground, and breathed into his nostrils the breath of life; and man became a living soul', Genesis 2:7.

Having declared that the whole face of the ground was watered by the mist that went up from the earth, Moses now shows how JEHOVAH Elohim formed the man that should till the ground. He was made of dust: 'And JEHOVAH Elohim formed man of the dust of the ground.'

This is the man that was made of dust. He is earthy. But how can this convey the image of God, who is spiritual, a Spirit? Because JEHOVAH Elohim 'breathed into his nostrils the breath of life'. Then man became 'a living soul', Genesis 2:7.

This breathing and living was not of the man. How could it have been? His formation was of the earth, earthy. The life of his soul stood in dependence on him whose breathing had quickened him into being, thereafter to sustain him, that by this he might live unto God.

Since it was not given to him to have life in himself, and because he had received life from above through his nostrils by the breathing of JEHOVAH Elohim, it behoved the man in all things to be subject to him on whose constant inbreathing he depended for life.

Man lived; but he was a living soul. His life was not within himself. It was from outside of himself. That is, he was not a being whose life was self-generating. He was formed from the clay, and then, far from life being created in him, it was passed to him from without.

Man was a lump of shaped clay, tremblingly dependent on this continual inbreathing of JEHOVAH Elohim from without to within, having no more means to sustain life within himself, than he had to quicken himself into being on the day of his creation. Then, without the least source of life from within, it became him to show forth all subjection to him that created him.

As to dominion over the earth, so swiftly was the woman to be deceived, drawing the man into the transgression, that no time elapsed for the fulfilment of such a charge.

And yet the man was made from the dust to till the ground. In this he was of the earth, earthy. And 'there went up a mist from the earth, and watered the whole face of the ground.' As Adam was formed from the ground, *Adamah*, so the mist was derived from the same earthy quarter.

'But there went up a mist from the earth, and watered the whole face of the ground', Genesis 2:6. In connection with the man came the mist. By its moisture he was to till the ground, and by this means the whole face of the ground was watered.

That is, the man formed from the dust of the ground, into whose nostrils the breath of life had been breathed, depended for his work upon that moisture which proceeded from the earth.

Since proceeding from the earth, however, was nothing other than what was true of himself, what other conclusion can be drawn than that despite the frailty of his being, withal his total dependence on his Creator for breath, *innately* Adam and his work did not stand in what came down from heaven, but in what went up from the earth?

His nature was that of a living soul, of the earth, earthy. His existence rested in the breathing of JEHOVAH. But the woman, being deceived, corrupted his innocence.

So long as he was entirely in dependence upon the breath which enervated his being from JEHOVAH Elohim, he was maintained in divine harmony. But the moment in which he—through the woman—so much as thought to depend on what was within himself, he was lost. He lost his life, and returned to the dust.

As opposed to the account of the creation of man in Genesis 1:27, that in chapter 2:7 teaches uniquely that man, formed from the dust of the ground, proceeding from the earth, was sustained by breath from above. Far from having strength or ability, man in innocence—let alone after the Fall—did not so much as possess life in and of himself.

He was dependent for life upon him who breathed into his nostrils the breath of life at the first. All that Adam in his innocence received was bestowed—lent—from above, and in this he found his being, his rest, and his happiness. So that what time in the garden—enticed by the woman—man looked to or for something from within himself, his fall was assured.

In himself, but dust and ashes, man had nothing. His very life was lent to him, and sustained for him, by JEHOVAH Elohim. Abiding in dependent subjection, he stood. But turning from his Maker to supposed knowledge and strength within himself in order to sustain his life independently, it was impossible for him to stand.

The Adversary—under a figure—approached the woman, and deceived her. It was she who succumbed to the lies and delusions of the Adversary. It is to be observed that the name Adam was given before the Fall. The name Eve was not. This was a name with a promise, given in prophecy, bestowed *after* the condemnation of the Fall, Genesis 3:20.

But, however deluded, the folly of the woman was in defiance both of Adam and of JEHOVAH Elohim. Through the woman, the man, following her in her enticements, knowingly defied his Maker, and brought down himself, his posterity, and the entire Creation.

Not so he whom the man had depicted, typified, and foreshadowed in the account of Creation in Genesis 1:26-28. Although the occasion was the forming of the first man Adam, yet in Genesis chapter 1 the purpose was to frame the account so that nothing was either included or excluded save that which resulted in pointing to Another, to the vision of the second Man, to the figure of Christ, the last Adam.

'And so it is written, The first man Adam was made a living soul; the last Adam was made a quickening spirit. Howbeit that was not first which is spiritual, but that which is natural; and afterward that which is spiritual. The first man is of the earth, earthy: the second man is the Lord from heaven', I Cor. 15:45-47.

Consider his long-awaited coming. He came as the Lord from heaven. That is, as the Word which was in the beginning, which was with God, and was God. All things were made by him: and without him was not anything made that was made. In him was life; and the life was the light of men. And the Word was made flesh.

Great is the mystery of godliness: God was manifest in the flesh. 'They shall call his name Emmanuel, which being interpreted is, God with us.' Withal God sent his Son, his Father being in heaven, yet the Father and the Son abode in divine unity, one in and with the Holy Ghost, One God, blessed for evermore.

The revelation of this mystery is great. It is of the essence in the new testament. Nevertheless we are not to intrude into it, or reason about it, but in faith to receive it. And worship. This is the mystery hidden from ages and generations; the mystery hidden in God—who created all things by Jesus Christ —from the foundation of the world.

When the fulness of time was come, God sent forth his Son, made of a woman, made under the law. He was made of the seed of David according to the flesh.

As to his birth, that is, the coming into the world of the Son from everlasting, lo, Mary was found with child of the Holy Ghost, for that which was conceived in her was of the Holy Ghost. Framed by the Holy Ghost in the womb of the virgin, here was that impeccable humanity—an utterly *new* humanity — which was assumed by the Son of God, the Lord from heaven, for ever to be his own.

When Mary asked, How shall this be, seeing I know not a man? It was told her, The Holy Ghost shall come upon thee, and the power of the Highest shall overshadow thee; therefore also that holy thing which shall be born of thee shall be called the Son of God.

That is, being in the form of God, the Son, who thought it not robbery to be equal with God, made himself of no reputation, and took upon him the form of a servant, and was made in the likeness of men, being found in fashion as a man.

Found in fashion as a man, yes, but it was not the same. This was the *second* Man. That is, the union in one of God and that unique Manhood, through the person of the Son, constituted the second Man. A new, a unique, heavenly order of humanity, wholly distinct from the first.

Hence Paul quotes from Genesis, the beginning of the old testament, and adds from the gospel, the beginning of the new testament, saying, 'And so it is written, The first man Adam was made a living soul; the last Adam was made a quickening spirit.'

The Son of God, the last Adam, is not said to have been made a living soul, observe. He is called a quickening spirit. That is, the first man had breath gratuitously breathed into his nostrils. Wherefore the life of that man was not *inherent*. It was imparted. Man *became* a living soul in the sense that he depended for life and breath from God *outside of himself.*

Of himself Adam was, and his posterity is, nothing but clay, and divinely formed clay at that. But the Son is not so. He is a quickening spirit, *being possessed of the divine nature, God himself withal.* However, being made of a woman, assuming human nature in union with his divine nature, though in his humanity wholly subject to the Father, still possessed of his own everlasting divine nature, and hence, *having life in himself.*

That is, the first man was of clay, and received human life from God's mere favour, gratuitously breathed from without into his nostrils. This was not, and is not, sustainable, without constant inbreathing. The consequence is termed 'a living soul'.

The second Man, being God himself, withal in his own unique humanity, has in virtue of his divinity the very essence of uncreated and eternal life in and of himself. For, saith John, 'the life was manifested, and we have seen it, and bear witness, and show unto you that eternal life, which was with the Father, and'—then coming into the world—'was manifested unto us.' Now, this is that life-giving, quickening spirit, called, The last Adam.

He is the brightness of God's glory, the express image of his person, and he is so in risen manhood. The manhood of the Son of God, that is, of the last Adam. His life, which is within himself, was not said—and could not be said—to have been created. It was said to have been *manifested*. That is, in his manhood, and by that manhood.

This is altogether other than the natural image of corruptible man, Rom. 1:23; it is wholly the spiritual image of the uncorruptible God. Whatever pale reflection of the image of God appeared in innocent Adam, in contrast the everlasting life, the eternal glory, the divine essence itself, shines out *from within himself* in the perfection of humanity in the Son of God, the second Man, the last Adam.

It is he who is the *express* image of God's person. He alone is the Man of God's purpose. Because he alone is the brightness of God's glory. Who else could be? whatever type, figure, or foreshadowing might have been designed of God, until the time was fulfilled? Only God manifest in the flesh, could in that flesh thus manifest God.

'Who is the image of the invisible God, the firstborn of every creature: for by him were all things created, that are in heaven, and that are in earth, visible and invisible, whether they be thrones, or dominions, or principalities, or powers: all things were created by him, and for him: and he is before all things, and by him all things consist', Col. 1:15-17.

At the appearing of our Lord Jesus Christ, in his times he shall show who is the blessed and only Potentate, the King of kings, and Lord of lords; who only hath immortality, dwelling in the light which no man can approach unto; whom—in his ascended glory—no man hath seen, nor can see: to whom be honour and power everlasting. Amen.

This shows the very nature of God. This shows the brightness of the glory of God. But all appears in the ascension of the Son *in manhood* to the right hand of the Father. Hence, beyond all question, this is the Man envisaged of God, foreshadowed by the first man, to whom all men should look, from the first man to the last. Because *this* Man, and this Man alone, *exactly conforms with Genesis 1:26-28.*

Although the second Man, Christ, is no mere living soul, but God himself withal, yet in his humiliation, in the days of his flesh, his subjection to his Father was wholly pleasing. It was altogether lovely. Of him on earth, the Father testified from heaven, This is my beloved Son, in whom I am well pleased.

He did nothing of himself. 'I can of mine own self do nothing.' He willed nothing of himself. 'I seek not mine own will, but the will of the Father which hath sent me.' He spoke nothing of himself. 'If I bear witness of myself, my witness is not true.' See John 5:30,31.

'For I have not spoken of myself; but the Father which sent me, he gave me a commandment, what I should say, and what I should speak. And I know that his commandment is life everlasting: whatsoever I speak therefore, even as the Father said unto me, so I speak', John 12:49,50.

He neither sought his own will, nor determined his own way. 'My meat is to do the will of him that sent me, and to finish his work', John 4:34. 'The Son can do nothing of himself, but what he seeth the Father do: for what things soever he doeth, these also doeth the Son likewise', John 5:19.

As to his own glory, that he laid aside, or ever he came into the world. 'And I seek not mine own glory: there is one that seeketh and judgeth', John 8:50. Could such things ever be said of Adam? But they can and must be said of the Son, in whom appears a perfect conformity to the man foreshadowed in Genesis 1:26-28.

Nevertheless, properly his unique Manhood is to be seen in resurrection glory, beyond death and the grave. It is at his Father's right hand, in light unapproachable, that the divine Manhood, the heavenly glory, of the second Man, and the last Adam, appears in its true character. And if in resurrection, then with a view to the world to come, whereof we speak.

There lies his coming dominion, for now we see not yet all things put under him. In this present world he was a stranger, a pilgrim, and a sojourner. Like Abraham before him, he looked for a city which hath foundations, whose builder and maker is God.

That city is new Jerusalem, which comes down from God out of heaven, prepared as a bride adorned for her husband. And the bride is one with her husband, bone of his bone, and flesh of his flesh, a stranger and pilgrim on the earth, desiring a better country, that is, an heavenly.

Of this holy city, new Jerusalem, and that better country, the world to come, the Son is heir. With it in view, the God of hope raised him from the dead. By the resurrection as heir of the heavenly inheritance, he is appointed to judge both quick and dead, henceforth to dissolve the very elements of this present world in fire at the last day.

'Looking for and hasting unto the coming of the day of God, wherein the heavens being on fire shall be dissolved, and the elements shall melt with fervent heat. Nevertheless we, according to his promise, look for new heavens and a new earth, wherein dwelleth righteousness', II Pet. 3:12,13.

And, said John, in the visions of God, 'I saw a new heaven and a new earth: for the first heaven and the first earth were passed away', Rev. 21:1. This is the everlasting inheritance and dominion of the Son, standing in the resurrection from the dead, after the last judgment, following the dissolution of all things pertaining to this present world.

It is to this, in a mystery—notwithstanding it be by the faintest of allusions—that the spiritual significance of Genesis 1:1 to 2:3 points the earnest seeker by the Holy Ghost from heaven. It is not to the first man or to his dominion of this present world. It is to the second Man, the risen Man, and to his dominion of that which is to come, world without end, Amen.

Just as two men, the first Adam and the last, the first man and the second, appear in the spiritual perception of Moses' narrative in Genesis 1 and 2, albeit in a hidden mystery, likewise their works, and the effect of them respectively, are mysteriously signified.

Observe the contrasting statements, Genesis 2:5, 'For JEHOVAH Elohim had not caused it to rain upon the earth', and, Genesis 2:6, 'But there went up a mist from the earth, and watered the whole face of the ground.' Two ways of moistening the ground without one or the other of which all would have withered and died.

But why mention the first? 'For JEHOVAH Elohim had not caused it to rain upon the earth.' But he did not cause it to do so until the Flood. So why mention what did not apply? Especially since the very next verse tells how the earth *was* watered *despite* the absence of rain? So why even mention the rain *when it did not apply?*

Because although it did not apply to *Adam* or how *he* wrought, it did point to *Christ* and how *he* would work. As to Adam, his work on earth was in virtue of the mist. This obtained throughout his lifetime. But the previous verse points to what Adam never experienced. It points to rain. And, in turn, this signifies the working of Christ.

In terms of rain *spiritually* there was not a man to till the ground until *he* came. Notice the verse: 'for JEHOVAH Elohim had not caused it to rain upon the earth, and there was not a man to till the ground.' But it did *not* rain; and a man to till the ground in *that* connection *never* appeared in the context of Genesis chapters 1 and 2.

However, mark the next verse: 'But there went up a mist from the earth.' But what has that to do with the rain just mentioned? It is an *alternative*. It is *another way* of giving moisture.

88

That is, for a *different* tiller of the ground, the one *first* to appear, that is, the first man Adam.

Just as rain, and a man, in that order, were conspicuous by their absence in Genesis 2:5, so mist and a man are most apparent by their presence in verses 6 and 7.

Ignoring what had been said immediately before—2:5—Moses tells us—2:6,7—that *mist* watered the earth, and in that connection straightway adds 'And JEHOVAH Elohim formed man of the dust of the ground'. This was the first man Adam.

What is the difference? Mist rises. But rain falls. The one goes up from the earth. The other comes down from heaven. There was no question here of any loss of Adam's original innocence, or of God's love for him, and pleasure in his work. It is simply a question of a man. The *first* man.

But for all that, this living soul was of the earth, earthy, formed from the dust of the ground. And his cultivation of the ground was in virtue of what went up from it: 'There went up a mist from the earth.' This proceeded from earth to heaven, and, like Adam, thereafter it fell.

Moses, who gave the law to Israel, also spoke of Christ. If he taught Israel of Adam, his work in the moisture of the mist, and his fall; he also prophesied of Christ, he foreshadowed his manhood, and he foretold of his coming. Said Christ to Israel, 'Had ye believed Moses, ye would have believed me: for he wrote of me.

'But if ye believe not his writings, how shall ye believe my words?', John 5:46,47.

Moses' writings were divinely given scriptures, telling of things old and new. Hence he says, 'My doctrine shall drop as the rain'—for example, in Genesis 1:1 to 2:3—'my speech shall distil as the dew'—notably, from Genesis 2:4 to 3:24—but Christ is seen first in the prophecy, and, Moses concludes, waiting for his coming, 'As the small rain upon the tender herb, and as the showers upon the grass', Deuteronomy 32:2.

Here notice that Moses refers to his *doctrine*. He compares *that* to rain and to dew. As to the rain, under such a figure Moses speaks of Christ in prophetic vision, and of the new testament in a hidden mystery.

As to the dew—which is akin to mist—Moses refers to his giving the law, and his promulgating the old covenant.

In the twain his doctrine was alike to both rain and dew. He brought forth out of his treasures—which he had received from God—things both old and new, between which none but the spiritual can distinguish, and which only the freeborn sons can tell apart.

Likewise the sweet psalmist of Israel, David, foretells of the coming of the promised Seed, which is Christ, the true son of David: 'He shall come down like rain upon the mown grass: as showers that water the earth', Psalm 72:6.

Similarly the prophet Isaiah confirms this word of truth: 'For as the rain cometh down, and the snow from heaven, and returneth not thither, but watereth the earth, and maketh it bring forth and bud, that it may give seed to the sower, and bread to the eater:

'So shall my word be that goeth forth out of my mouth: it shall not return unto me void, but it shall accomplish that which I please, and it shall prosper in the thing whereto I sent it', Isaiah 55:10,11.

This is what is experienced in Christ, and under the new testament. It is like the rain from heaven, like showers from above. Nothing can better describe this experimental refreshment from Christ in the heavenly word of the truth of the gospel. It signifies his present spiritual work, for now the LORD God *hath* caused it to rain upon the earth.

But that which comes down from heaven shall not fully be realized until he comes again. For he cometh, he cometh to judge the earth: with righteousness shall he judge the world, and the people with equity.

'But the day of the Lord will come as a thief in the night; in the which the heavens shall pass away with a great noise, and the elements shall melt with fervent heat, the earth also and the works that are therein shall be burned up', II Pet. 3:10.

This heralds the falling of the rain from heaven, beyond rapture to tell, upon his own people, the fruit of his sowing: 'For the Lord *himself* shall descend from heaven with a shout, with the voice of the archangel, and with the trump of God: and the dead in Christ shall rise first:

'Then we which are alive and remain shall be caught up together with them in the clouds, to meet the Lord in the air: and so shall we ever be with the Lord', I Thessalonians 4:16,17. This is to pour water upon him that is thirsty, and floods upon the dry ground: I will pour my spirit upon thy seed, and my blessing upon thine offspring, Isa. 44:3.

'Behold', cries John, 'he cometh with clouds.' Now these are the spiritual clouds, that herald the rain, and shall reveal the Man, the second Man, the last Adam, who once tilled the ground, and once sowed the seed, but is now come for his harvest.

'Behold, he cometh with clouds; and every eye shall see him, and they also which pierced him: and all kindreds of the earth shall wail because of him. Even so, Amen', Revelation 1:7.

'He which testifieth these things saith, Surely I come quickly. Amen. Even so, come, Lord Jesus. The grace of our Lord Jesus Christ be with you all. Amen.'

IV

The River in Eden

JEHOVAH Elohim — translated 'the LORD God' in the Authorized Version—formed man of the dust of the ground, and breathed into his nostrils the breath of life; and man became a living soul, Genesis 2:7.

Straightway the narrative continues with the unfolding of the counsels of JEHOVAH Elohim, revealed to and laid up for the first man Adam. This begins with the planting of a garden.

It was not that Adam planted the garden, or that he had received directions or was instructed to do so. It was JEHOVAH Elohim that planted the garden.

'And the LORD God planted a garden eastward in Eden; and there he put the man whom he had formed', Genesis 2:8. Hitherto the earth had been spoken of in a general way. Now, with the creation of Adam, the reference becomes particular.

It was not a matter of the habitation of the earth generally: that followed later. Here it was a question of the situation of the first man Adam. If so, of one place. The questions arise, Where was that place; and what distinguished it?

First, the place was in Eden. Next, what distinguished it was the planting of JEHOVAH Elohim. '*There* he put the man whom he had formed.' It was not simply Eden. Eden was larger than the garden. The garden was part of Eden. 'The LORD God planted a garden *eastward* in Eden.'

Eden was not the garden. The garden was in Eden. It was called The Garden of Eden, but it occupied the east only. Eden itself stretched to the north, south, east, and west. This area was above and beyond the garden which JEHOVAH Elohim had planted '*Eastward* in Eden', Genesis 2:8.

Whilst the passage is mystical—as are both the ELOHIM and JEHOVAH Elohim accounts of the Creation—nevertheless everything rests on facts. Discernment lies in perceiving that the facts included or excluded point to divine mysteries. The interpretation of such mysteries is revealed by the Holy Ghost. There is no understanding without the Spirit.

Many carnal men, uncalled and unsent, blunder in the meaning.

For example, taking the passage 'A garden inclosed is my sister, my spouse', such blind leaders of the blind conclude that the 'garden' of Eden is therefore a figure of Christ and the Church, his spouse. But how can that possibly be in the case of the garden of Eden?

At that time the type of the spouse—Eve—was not so much as in existence. How then could the garden answer to a figure that did not exist? Besides, the place reads 'There he put *the man* whom he had formed', Genesis 2:8.

Others say that the garden of Eden was the vineyard of JEHOVAH's planting. But, for one thing, the figure of the vineyard was reserved for Israel alone, and for another, the parable tells us that the vineyard was 'let out to husbandmen', plural, not Adam, singular. As to the husbandmen, they are called 'the chief priests and Pharisees', Mt. 21:45.

In the garden of Eden Adam tilled alone; 'husbandmen' were non-existent; no 'vineyard' is mentioned; and even the mere concept of Israel lay beyond the Deluge, long after the revelation of God's choice of Abraham.

The scripture teaches, however, that JEHOVAH Elohim wrought beforehand in Eden. The garden to the east of Eden had already been planted in advance of Adam's arrival. 'And JEHOVAH Elohim planted a garden eastward in Eden; and there he put the man whom he had formed', Genesis 2:8.

When man was formed, the work had been done: the garden was already planted. Adam was introduced to that which JEHOVAH Elohim had prepared and reserved for him. Throughout it was a question of what JEHOVAH Elohim initiated. It was not what man did for JEHOVAH Elohim: it was what JEHOVAH Elohim did for man.

Everything was purposed and conceived in the prior counsel and work of JEHOVAH Elohim. For this, Adam was created. Into it, he was brought. JEHOVAH Elohim *put* the man whom he had formed in the garden which he had planted.

But why? Because in the garden Adam would behold the visible expression of the mind of JEHOVAH Elohim for the cultivation of the earth. Here a divine precedent had been established; here JEHOVAH Elohim himself had set forth that which brought to perfection every element of Creation. And here he put the man whom he had formed.

JEHOVAH Elohim had taken the initiative, not only in the Creation, but in that planting which would bring to light the beauty, order, and consummation latent in the *cultivation* of all that he had created and made. Here he put the man. Here the man saw to a demonstration why he had been set down in the garden of Eden.

In the meek and glad submission which became the man whom JEHOVAH Elohim had formed from the dust of the ground, quickening and sustaining him by the breath of his mouth, Adam was not only to respond with worship and gratitude for that eternal power and Godhead revealed in

Creation itself, but he was to answer in service to the expression of the divine mind seen in the planting of the garden.

The man was to observe the way in which, and with what, the garden had been planted, and how it was to be maintained, henceforth to preserve that pristine arrangement in its original beauty. More, having perceived—not simply the effect of the divine work, but — the *method* of work, and the *work itself*, which such a vista set before his eyes, from his heart he would be moved to exemplify his Maker.

In a sense this heart language, spontaneously springing to his lips, was a foreshadowing of the Son with the Father. Only, the earthy man would say not over things spiritual, but things natural, 'JEHOVAH Elohim worketh hitherto, and I work'.

And again a sense of him whom he typified might be found by adapting and applying the words in retrospection—but with perfect equity—in that Adam, fulfilled, could say, 'My meat is to do the will of him that formed me, and to finish his work.'

For that work of divine planting demonstrated to man not just the service but the *very principles and method of it*, by which he should glorify JEHOVAH Elohim through its increase.

As JEHOVAH Elohim had planted, so he was to plant. As JEHOVAH Elohim had laid out the garden eastward in Eden, so he was to extend that garden throughout Eden. As JEHOVAH Elohim showed the knowledge of his glory in a prospect, so he was to realize that vision, till the earth should be filled with the knowledge of the glory of JEHOVAH, as the waters cover the sea.

Thus the thought and intent of JEHOVAH Elohim for man appears in this passage and context. According to the landscape — the delightful beauty and arrangement — of the garden of JEHOVAH Elohim's planting, so man should constantly defer to him, ever responding to his inbreathing, answering to his initiative, keeping and increasing the work of God to the glory of JEHOVAH.

For this was the design of the garden, that as JEHOVAH Elohim had wrought, and as men multiplied, so his work, and the knowledge and glory of it, should expand and fructify. 'And a river went out of Eden.' This was 'to water the garden.' But it was far more: 'and from thence it was parted, and became into four heads', Genesis 2:10.

Ever flowing, ever increasing, ever branching—to the four corners of the earth, even to the world's ends — carrying the blessing and increase of the knowledge of the glory of God. Such were God's thoughts, and as evidently they were expressed.

The seeds of the planting of JEHOVAH Elohim should be carried out in their seasons upon the waters and throughout the branches of the river. Tilled by man in subjection to JEHOVAH Elohim, working out from the banks of the river and its four heads, through man's responsive service in answer to the divine planting, the blessing should be spread abroad, thence to the regions beyond.

The vision, brightening from the boundaries of the garden of Eden, beyond Eden, reaching past all imagination, shone on a scene of perfection, order, and beauty vastly beyond the horizon. The whole earth should be one garden of delight, a scene of perfect harmony between heaven and earth, earth and heaven, JEHOVAH Elohim and man, Adam and his Maker.

Far beyond the garden lay this bright hope. It was the glory that shone in the expectation of the man, exceeding all the limits of the place in which he had been put. It was within him to see beyond, to be inspired by a vision of Creation, a harmony of the creature, in which the whole earth should be dressed and kept even as the garden of JEHOVAH.

Of this the garden of Eden spoke to Adam, so remarkable in his insight, discernment, and vision. If so, nothing of the location of the garden would have been lost on the man so distinctive in that humanity proceeding from the hand and breath of JEHOVAH Elohim.

'And the LORD God planted a garden *eastward* in Eden', Genesis 2:8. Here is an exact location. Here JEHOVAH Elohim chose to locate, and wrought to plant, the garden of Eden. The present location—even if it could be estimated since the Fall and after the universal destruction of the Flood, which it cannot—is immaterial.

What is material is the revelation of the work of JEHOVAH Elohim in his choice and planting of the garden. For, these things being accomplished, *there* he put the man whom he had formed. Such precision is involved: there he *put* the man. Then, the place affords doctrine in itself, the significance of which ought to be grasped and savoured.

First the garden was in Eden. This is in fact a Hebrew word, carried over—or transliterated—in the English bible without having been translated. However the meaning is Delight, or Pleasure. So that those who suppose the sovereign exercise of the will of the LORD God to be connected with inexorable rigour and unmitigated misery are sorely mistaken. They greatly err.

The very name Eden means Pleasure. And if so, for whom? It was not named for JEHOVAH Elohim. It was named for man. Then, by JEHOVAH Elohim. If so, where is this unbearable yoke, this wretched servitude, this despotic rule, that unbelievers conjure? Here is no cold, hard regimen; here no remote Despot willing and taking pleasure in man's slavish fear and misery.

Eden gives the lie to such distortions. Eden is the very epitome of divine joy in giving freely of his own delight and pleasure to accompany man's happiness in the fulfilment of his destiny.

The placing of Adam in the garden of delights, there to answer to the working and planting of JEHOVAH Elohim, fellow-labouring with all meekness and submission, discerning and practising with every pleasure the things exemplified in the planting of the LORD God: Here lay true happiness!

Worshipping the Creator; perceiving in the things created and made even his eternal power and Godhead; enraptured by such union and harmony between heaven and earth, God and man: what bliss could be comparable? The more so, to one who of himself was but dust and ashes.

And shall JEHOVAH Elohim show his own eternal goodness, his very nature of love, and breathe into man's nostrils the breath of life, constantly sustaining both breath and life, then, withal, putting man in the garden afore prepared for him, filled with all manner of trees for beauty and food, and calling it Delight and Pleasure?

Nor is this all that JEHOVAH Elohim had prepared for man. For it is written, 'The LORD God planted a garden *eastward* in Eden', Genesis 2:8. By which it is evident that not only was a sense of direction bestowed upon Adam, but also of perspective.

Then, through these things without, and the spirit of man within, besides the splintering of a thousand rays in the prism of God's word and Creation, Adam in innocence knew of a certainty that *this* was not the *ultimate* fulfilment of God's purpose, *and nor was he.*

The garden in which Adam had been put was eastward. Immediately such an aspect referred the man to the place from whence light breaks forth: from the East. As if to say daily, More light is to come.

Nor was this all. But at this time I say nothing of the Tree of Life. However, even in the midst of the garden Adam would have perceived that the life was the light of men.

If so, more light—let alone life—must be to come. As with the rising of the sun light broke forth from the east, so surely —and centrally—stood the testimony that the Life should be manifested in his own times.

Evidently displayed before Adam's eyes; clearly perceived in his experimental providences; obviously portrayed in sign after sign: Adam *knew* he should look for, and trust in, that which was promised, a vision to be revealed in the good pleasure and will of JEHOVAH Elohim when the fulness of time was come.

That is, Adam in his innocence was taught even from the first opening of his eyes that neither he nor this Creation constituted the full revelation of God's purpose: there was the promise of that purpose. The consummation was neither full nor complete.

Little may have been fully perceived. Much must have been innocently trusted. One thing was certain, morning by morning it appeared: *more light was to come.*

The very orientation of the garden would draw the man at the dawning of every day to the first beams of light filtering through the trees, tracing the leaves, shafting across the open spaces, till, blazing with glory, for a sign in the heavens—'Let them be for signs', Genesis 1:14—a figure of the coming Sun of righteousness arose, with healing in his beams.

For the LORD God is a sun and shield: no good thing will he withhold from them that walk uprightly. And would no knowledge at all have come to Adam through him by whom the world was made, that '*I* am the light of the world'? If not, how could it have been said that 'The *life* was the light of men'?

100

The kindness of JEHOVAH Elohim to Adam in his innocence, whilst not manifesting the coming Son of God, certainly showed that—as the east itself displayed morning by morning—*light was to break forth*. More light was to come.

Alas, all this was to be shattered. Adam's transgression—so soon—brought in the darkness of the Fall with its catastrophic enormities upon the whole world. But as yet, Genesis 2:8, the man stood in innocence, guileless eyes in the morning of time facing the breaking forth of the light eastward in Eden.

But this was a figure. Yet more revealing was the figure of the tree of Life. Not the tree of Light, the tree of Life.

For in every figure, all the light shone from *him* who was promised, for whom man was to wait, and to whose coming the whole of time deferred. Indeed, it was to the Man of God's purpose that all Creation pointed, and concerning whom even Adam himself provided the figure.

The Second Man, the Last Adam, that quickening Spirit, shed abroad the beams of his promised rising, and to this, as to the breaking of the day, Eden looked. 'And he shall be as the light of the morning, when the sun riseth, even a morning without clouds; as the tender grass springing out of the earth by clear shining after rain.'

Eden itself bore witness by a sign: all the light had not yet been revealed; all the life had not yet been manifested. It was anticipatory of light and life that the garden was eastward in Eden, and that the tree of life—which was the light of men— was in the midst of the garden.

Thus Christ, who was before all, was set before all in a figure, even from the dawn of time. Had Adam trusted in him, and looked steadfastly for his coming, watching for the morning yet to dawn with the rising of the true light, all had been fulfilled that was so full of promise and hope when, eastward in Eden, JEHOVAH Elohim 'put the man whom he had formed'.

That is, JEHOVAH Elohim put the man in the place which by his *own* divine planting *he* had laid out for him, a place of beauty and adornment, a place called Pleasure and Delight. Here was a place, a garden, in which *every* tree—such variety!— vied one with the other for pleasantness of sight, and delectability of taste. There, there he put the man whom he had formed.

By this very lovingkindness, all deity conspired to protest that all that proceeded from him for man was lovely, harmonious, and balanced to perfection, being summed up in the word 'Delight'. By such incontrovertible tokens JEHOVAH Elohim cannot conceivably have been the author of the Fall; nor yet could he have intended it. These things proceeded not from him.

He is not the instigator of sin; of corruption; of the curse; or of darkness and death. Execute judgment he must: but instigate transgression he cannot. Indeed, there is none good but God, and all goodness — and nothing but goodness — of necessity flows from him without cessation. All that he brought in was good, it was very good, and everything was exceeding beautiful.

Therefore it is nothing other than blasphemy against all that he created, and all that Creation showed of him, to invent evil imaginings presupposing that man evolved from a series of grotesque and primitive organisms. The truth is that 'JEHOVAH Elohim formed man of the dust of the ground, and breathed into his nostrils the breath of life; and man became a living soul', Genesis 2:7.

This living soul, directly created, is called, 'The man whom *he* had formed', Genesis 2:8. And formed for glory and for beauty.

So was the garden of Eden to look upon. It was not that the hideous was refined to become lovely. Loveliness was *created at the beginning*. Decay, degeneration, and death are the immutable rules of fallen nature. The very opposite pertains to every divine Creation.

Man, the transgressor, and the woman, the deceived, cast *themselves* into the darkness and death of sin and the grave. But it was not so from the beginning. However—now—in the inward darkness of the Fall man can no longer see the beginning, much less can he conceive of him who in the beginning created the heaven and the earth.

Behind the blackness of darkness man's depraved mind blindly imagines a remote, cold, hostile force—call it God— implacably set in malign hostility to mankind. But, like the deception; the transgression; the Fall; the curse; the decay; the darkness; and death itself, all these are things caused by and maintained through Satan.

This false conception of God is from Satan, who was a liar from the beginning. It was *his* covetousness that inflamed the woman, who enticed the man, and this was what caused mankind to pass under the dominion of the Adversary. 'Ye are of your father the devil, and the lusts of your father ye will do.

'He was a murderer from the beginning'—who in the beginning murdered both our living souls, and our brotherly love— 'He was a murderer from the beginning, and abode not in the truth, because there is no truth in him. When he speaketh a lie, he speaketh of his own: for he is a liar, and the father of it', John 8:44.

Seeing therefore that nothing but good came from the LORD God, it can never be said—nor ought it once to be thought— that God willed the Fall so that by it his eternal purpose in Christ might come to light. God did *not* will the Fall, but did all to prevent it, encouraging man in innocence to look for and trust in Christ in type, figure, shadow, promise, and prophecy.

But *man* would not. The truth is, both under his name ELOHIM, and that of JEHOVAH Elohim, *God promised Christ before the Fall*, and hence that promise *could not be dependent upon the Fall*. There can be no doubt of the promise irrespective of the conduct of Adam.

That Adam fell was due entirely to Satan as the cause, and man as the sinner. Now therefore the grace of God radiates the more abundantly in that despite the universal rebellion of man in Adam, *the promise apparent even before the Fall still holds good*, and, at that, *by way of redemption then beyond the heart and mind of man to conceive.*

As to God, his way is perfect, and this is the more conspicuous in the blessing and delight conceived for the happiness of man. *There* he put the man whom he had formed.

'And out of the ground made JEHOVAH Elohim to grow every tree that is pleasant to the sight, and good for food', Genesis 2:9. To defer comment at this time on the tree of life, and the tree of the knowledge of good and evil, here is a scene of exquisite loveliness and of the most abundant bounty.

Observe; 'Out of the ground *made* JEHOVAH Elohim to grow *every* tree that is pleasant to the sight, and good for food.' It is as if the LORD God delighted to exert that creative power unique to himself—he *made* to grow—to show forth such prolific liberality—*every* tree—for the delight of man.

Everything that JEHOVAH Elohim created, formed, caused, or wrought, it was the same: goodness and abundance over-flowed, life and beauty multiplied. And all this, mark, for man's blessing. Nothing was stinted; there was no *hint* of mean or stringent necessity: everything superabounded; all was of the most lavish plenitude.

The entire garden was full of beauty; all the trees were pleasant; the entire prospect was one of loveliness; every provision was delightful; each aspect contributed its own comeliness. It was upon such things that man was formed to look; in such an environment that he was put to serve; and from such perfection of provision that he was given to be nourished.

Adam was to ponder Jehovah's planting. He was to look upon whatsoever things were true; whatsoever things were honest; whatsoever things were just; whatsoever things were pure; whatsoever things were lovely; whatsoever things were of good report: if there were any virtue, if there were any praise, upon this Adam was to meditate. And, in pristine Creation, to purest innocence, What else *should* exist?

Not only did Jehovah Elohim delight to enrich — even enrapture—with such manifestations of his divine goodness, but he *willed* to do so: it was his *desire* that Adam should enjoy such an abundance in the garden of Delight, knowing his love for man.

Even the provision of food—so lowly a matter in such a divine context—expressed the care and solicitude of Jehovah Elohim down to the very hairs upon the head of man. He gave Adam to consume no mere bread and water, but *every* tree that was *good* for food.

Nothing was eked out: niggardliness was unknown. Only that man had what was good. No good thing was withheld from the man whom Jehovah Elohim had formed, who walked in his innocence.

Then where is this doctrine of devils that parodies man as if evolving from some moron-like ape, scraping a pit of moss for grubs, tearing with bloody hands at some gory carcase? Where is this damnable conjuring of some half-bestial creature, aimlessly wandering in a hideous wilderness, or floundering in some monstrous swamp?

Where? And where the primitive gruntings, the purposeless meanderings, the dread fear of a something, little more than an alien force in the dark, working against man, and against whom man must work to survive his meaningless span? Where? Nowhere but in the lies of Satan ingrained in the depraved mind of man in the darkness of the Fall.

Where? Nowhere. Nowhere at all. Nowhere on earth. Nowhere in heaven. Nowhere in time. Nowhere in Eden. Only with the father of lies, who abode not in the truth, who, when he speaketh a lie, speaketh of his own: for he is a liar, and the father of it. And yet this is the poisonous venom that courses through the life-blood and being of humanity since the Fall.

The truth is, JEHOVAH Elohim planted a garden eastward in Eden; and *there* he put the man whom *he* had formed—and formed immediately and instantly, and formed in the perfection of innocence—Genesis 2:8.

The Hebrew word translated 'put', gives the idea of 'to appoint', 'cause to be', 'to set', 'to place'. It is indicative of a divine action of immense kindness to Adam—who is regarded as passive—to settle him down in the place prepared.

But the Hebrew of Genesis 2:8 is not the same as the word translated 'put' in Genesis 2:15. 'And JEHOVAH Elohim took the man, and *put* him into the garden of Eden to dress it and to keep it', Gen. 2:15. Not the same at all: indeed, as opposed to the context of 'put' in verse 8, in Genesis 2:15 Adam's being 'put' is in consequence of his first having been 'taken'.

The cause of Adam's being 'put' into the garden, according to Genesis 2:15, occurred when JEHOVAH Elohim 'took' the man. This implies his being taken up, conveyed, and brought —at least—over some distance.

The suggestion is that the man, newly created, alive, intelligent, would certainly be quick to perceive the wonders about him, and those of the Creator who made him. What effect then, the sharp contrast of being 'taken' to the divinely planted garden?

Comparing the place of his creation with the garden of God's preparation, immediately Adam would perceive how marvellous was the unfolding love and provision of his Maker.

Having been 'taken'—from the place of his creation—Adam was 'put into' the garden of Eden, Genesis 2:15.

Although two separate words in the original have both been translated by the one word 'put' in the English, the meaning of the Hebrew word in verse 8 differs from that in verse 15. The original in verse 15 conveys a different sense. 'Put into' conveys the idea of rest, of a resting place, of being caused to rest, of being laid down in the place prepared and suited for an habitation.

But there is a purpose. Jᴇʜᴏᴠᴀʜ Elohim *took* Adam, he *caused him to rest* in the garden, so that the fulfilment of the life and energy of Adam would appear before his eyes. He would behold what was agreeable to every instinct of his being. To his delight, who had been brought and situated, what was now before him exactly suited his nature and aspiration.

Taken, put into, the garden, Adam was 'to dress it and to keep it', Genesis 2:15. The word 'dress' is most deceptive, and indicates more of the prejudice of the translators than it does the significance of the Hebrew. The Hebrew is *Abad*. It is not the first occurrence of this word.

Abad occurs first in Genesis 2:5, 'There was not a man to *till* the ground.' Omitting the verse in question, Genesis 2:15, the next reference appears after the Fall of Adam. 'Therefore JEHOVAH Elohim sent him forth from the garden of Eden, to *till* the ground from whence he was taken. So he drove out the man', Genesis 3:23.

The English word used most frequently to translate *Abad*— two hundred and fourteen times—is 'serve'. The next most frequent—six times—is 'till'. After that there is a various scattering of English words all supposed to convey the meaning of this one Hebrew word. Among this scattering *Abad* has been translated 'dress' twice.

The first of these occurrences appears in Genesis 2:15. This verse *should* read, 'And JEHOVAH Elohim took the man, and put him into the garden of Eden *to till it* and to keep it.'

Adam, discerning and answering to the planting of God, was to take the part of a fellowlabourer, in humble submission to the divine principles and methods revealed, *to extend that work*. And to *keep* what had been extended.

To keep, heed, maintain what JEHOVAH Elohim had planted, and, precisely according to his ways, to extend it; next to keep that; thereafter, as a wondrous prospect for humanity, to carry outwards and sustain the ground cultivated, even to the uttermost parts of the earth. That was the hope.

But how should man extend? By following the river, and its four heads, irrigating, planting, and extending from the banks. This is clearly implied in the context. And beyond both context and implication, faintly there may be traced a prophetic, a spiritual, heavenly, mysterious, and divine shadow of the things of Christ with a view to the world to come.

Observe the text and context, indicative of such hope set before Adam and his seed in innocence, by the providence of JEHOVAH Elohim.

'And a river went out of Eden'—mark that: not out of the garden of Eden to the eastward; but out of Eden eastward to the garden—'to water the garden'. By this watering, by such a divine irrigation, by a kind of necessity Adam would increase the work of planting.

How? 'And from thence it was parted, and became into four heads.' From whence? Not whence it came, which was Eden; but whence it watered, which was the garden. From *thence* it was parted and became into four heads.

'The name of the first is Pison: that is it which compasseth the whole land of Havilah, where there is gold; and the gold of that land is good: there is bdellium and the onyx stone.

'And the name of the second river is Gihon: the same is it that compasseth the whole land of Ethiopia.

'And the name of the third river is Hiddekel: that is it which goeth toward the east of Assyria. And the fourth river is Euphrates', Genesis 2:10-14.

To seek for the locations of these rivers—or for the matter of that, for Eden—is futile. The names and places are not recorded for *that* purpose, but rather to teach doctrine.

In any event, so cataclysmic was the universal Deluge, from the heights of heaven to the fountains of the deep; so overwhelming the changes over the face of the whole earth; and so prolonged the prevailing period of the Flood, *that no antediluvian features bear any relation to present conditions, and few, if any, places can bear even the most approximate geographical comparison despite the subsequent duplication of antediluvian names.*

In the record of the four 'heads', Genesis 2:10-14, information decreases in proportion to the successive mention of each river. In the first case, Pison, the entire reach of the river is traced, its territory named, and not only so, but the riches of the land in both precious metal and stones is discovered.

In the second case, Gihon, the whole stretch of the river is described, with the land that it encompasses, but no more. In the third, Hiddekel, mention is made of nothing save the land direction in which this river becomes lost to view. In the last case, only the name of the river is mentioned.

It was as if it were proposed that the four great waters—or the heads of the river flowing out of Eden—should have been systematically navigated, and that with the intention of exploring the land which each encompassed.

Seemingly fully achieved at the first, the success of this objective progressively diminished, till at the last, discovery failed. At the consecutive mention of each of the four rivers less and less is said, till at length nothing can be said, save that *this* was the name of the remaining river.

Not that Adam knew such things, or could have known them. But the Holy Ghost knew, and the record is indicative of *what was there*, had man but pursued the hope that was set before him in his heritage of the dominion of the earth, and increase of the garden of JEHOVAH Elohim, in the way that was exemplified before him in vision.

In the event, everything lost for ever, the condemnation upon Adam and his posterity, the curse over all the earth, irrevocably excluded from Eden, fallen man might indeed trace the courses of the rivers—till the universal Flood—but he had lost both source and direction world without end.

And yet—alas—how much hope; how much prosperity; how much vision had been promised even in the names of the rivers. Proceeding from Eden—Delight or Pleasure—to water the garden, the first river by interpretation meant 'Freely flowing'. The second, 'Stream'. The third, 'Rapid'. And the last, 'Bursting'.

Indicating in succession the Source; the Issue; the Outpouring; and the Abundance, What more could have drawn man to be fruitful, to multiply, to replenish the earth, and to subdue it?

Given the example of the planting of JEHOVAH Elohim, of the river from Eden watering the garden, what greater incentive could have existed than the divergence of the four flowing heads to bring forward the work of the Creator, even to the ends of the earth? But this never happened. To man, and in this present world, it is lost for ever.

Nevertheless nothing of God can be lost. The realization of the vision and hope lay in Another; in a second Man; in the last Adam. It lay in a new Creation; in the world to come; in spiritual fulfilment in the new heavens and the new earth.

It is not that everything is lost. It is that Adam and his posterity lost everything. But God has lost nothing. And all that Adam lost, in a far higher, transcendent, spiritual way, Christ has gained superabundantly for his God and Father in everlasting life in an eternal inheritance world without end.

It is not that defeat, despair, and irrevocable loss appear in the unfolding of the revelation of God. As the scriptures progressively reveal the purpose of God, more and more, Christ being foretold, and his destiny made known, it is victory, hope, and sure expectation that burst forth with joy in the unfolding prophecy.

Although man has lost the river of God in the Fall, and Adam has been driven out of the garden of Eden never to return, yet, despite the vast destruction of the Deluge—altering irrevocably even the original geographical features of Eden and the entire old world—*nothing is lost in the purpose of God.*

Nothing is lost. Rather, the gain in Christ exceeds the loss in Adam, as high as the heavens exceed in height above the earth. It is true that man has lost the river of God, but it is just as true that God has retained it, that Christ has regained it, and that the gospel has elevated it.

The scriptures of the prophets, the words of Jesus, and the doctrine of the apostles, all manifest the transcendent spiritual elevation of a lost river that proved at last to be no more than a shadow, a type: nothing but a figure. A figure, that is, of all that is in Christ, of everything that is for the world to come, and of the outflowing that pertains for ever to the world that shall abide to everlasting.

So the scriptures unfold. Under the old legal covenant, by the word of JEHOVAH Elohim, Moses led the people through the Red Sea, into the waste howling wilderness wherein there was no water.

'Wherefore the people did chide with Moses, and said, Give us water that we may drink. And Moses said unto them, Why chide ye with me? wherefore do ye tempt JEHOVAH?

'And the people thirsted there for water; and the people murmured against Moses, and said, Wherefore is this that thou hast brought us up out of Egypt, to kill us and our children and our cattle with thirst?

'And Moses cried unto JEHOVAH, saying, What shall I do unto this people? they be almost ready to stone me. And JEHOVAH said unto Moses, Go on before the people, and take with thee of the elders of Israel; and thy rod, wherewith thou smotest the river, take in thine hand, and go.

'Behold, I will stand before thee there upon the rock in Horeb; and thou shalt smite the rock, and there shall come water out of it, that the people may drink. And Moses did so in the sight of the elders of Israel', Exodus 17:2-6.

As to Moses, the law was given by Moses. As for the people, chosen or not as a nation, they were—as saith JEHOVAH Elohim —of the fallen seed of Adam, cast out of the garden, banished from the river, under the curse, and beneath the sentence of death. And all this they confirmed in themselves time out of number, rebelling again and again, filling up the measure of their iniquity, transgression, and sin.

For their sin they were without water. For their unbelief they had no drink. But Moses, who gave the law, pronounced the curse; and how should justice be served if mercy were abused? They did not *deserve* water, any more than their father Adam: they *deserved* punishment, as did their father Adam. It was the *obligation* of the lawgiver, Moses, to execute vengeance.

But God would have mercy. Only he would have justice also, and magnify the law, and make it honourable in their sight. Moses therefore was to take his rod: the lawgiver was to insist upon its sanctions. The stripes of Moses' rod must fall to meet the just demands of the broken law. The curse must fall.

Then shall the people for ever wander, to die of thirst? Justly yes. Legally, that was right. But mercifully, no. Graciously, righteousness might be fulfilled in another way. Moses stood before the rock. He lifted the rod of his wrath, the curse of the law. But '*I* will stand before thee there upon the rock in Horeb; and thou shalt smite the rock.'

Then, when Moses brought down the rod of legal wrath to execute the curse of the law, before in its descent it fell upon and smote the rock itself, it must needs sweep the arc of its full force through him who stood upon the rock before Moses. '*I* will stand before thee there upon on the rock.'

If so, to smite the rock, Moses, the law, the rod of the wrath and punishment of the curse, must first smite *him who stood upon it.* This executed the judgment: but it was upon Another,

113

a willing Substitute. Justice satisfied; righteousness fulfilled; mercy flowed; and the waters gushed forth.

Albeit invisibly, JEHOVAH stood, and JEHOVAH took the full force of the blow due to the lawless people, or ever the curse expended its force upon the smitten rock. 'Christ hath redeemed us from the curse of the law, being made a curse for us', Gal. 3:13. Or, in another place, 'That Rock was Christ.'

'He clave the rocks in the wilderness, and gave them drink as out of the great depths. He brought streams also out of the rock, and caused waters to run down like rivers', Psalm 78:15,16. And again, 'Which turned the rock into a standing water, the flint into a fountain of waters', Psalm 114:8.

'He opened the rock, and the waters gushed out; they ran in the dry places like a river', Psalm 105:41. Is not this water enough to till the ground? 'Thou visitest the earth, and waterest it: thou greatly enrichest it with the river of God, which is full of water: thou preparest them corn, when thou hast so provided for it.

'Thou waterest the ridges thereof abundantly: thou settlest the furrows thereof: thou makest it soft with showers: thou blessest the springing thereof', Psalm 65:9,10.

And if any complain that such water is of nature; or that there is no allusion to the Spirit in these things: if one object that all this belongs to men and this Creation, to natural water; that such things do not foreshadow Christ and the world to come, or spiritual water, then, Let the apostle Paul answer:

'Moreover, brethren, I would not that ye should be ignorant, how that all our fathers were under the cloud, and all passed through the sea; and were all baptized unto Moses in the cloud and in the sea; and did all eat the same spiritual meat.'

'And *did all drink the same spiritual drink.*' You observe that? *Spiritual* drink: 'for they drank of that *spiritual* Rock.' You note it? *Spiritual* Rock: 'drank of that spiritual Rock that followed them: and that Rock was Christ', I Corinthians 10:1-4.

Then will any tell me that this water was not a foreshadowing? that it had no spiritual significance? that it was not *full* of spiritual allusion? *Full of Christ?* That is, of *waters* from Christ's fulness?

Consider this unfolding revelation opening up throughout the old testament. For that which was natural, which had been lost in Adam, yet in the counsels of God foreshadowed and signified those things which are spiritual, the things which should be gained in Christ.

For in sundry ways and divers manners, whether by type, shadow, prophecy, or figure, the promise of God in the scriptures gathered up the golden threads of divine witness to foretell of better things to come.

These things are likewise signified even in the day of the destruction of Jerusalem, when the house of God, the temple of the LORD, was razed to the foundations thereof. As it was in the day that Adam fell, and the curse descended upon man and his posterity, being cast out of Eden, beyond reach of the tree of life or the river of God for ever, so it appeared in the day of Jerusalem's destruction.

But in the fourteenth year after that the city was smitten, in the selfsame day, the hand of JEHOVAH was upon Ezekiel the prophet as he lay in captivity in far-off Babylon, 'and he brought me thither', Ezekiel 40:1.

'In the visions of God brought he me into the land of Israel, and set me upon a very high mountain, by which was as the frame of a city on the south.'

To the chosen prophet the supernatural mystery unfolds from the fortieth to the forty-seventh chapters. From the heights of glory appears the mystical revelation of another city, an heavenly, a new Jerusalem, with another house of God, which is the *ecclesia* of the living God, the pillar and ground of the truth. 'Destroy this temple, and in three days I will raise it up.'

Divine; mysterious; incomprehensible; heavenly; glorious; visionary; spiritual: so the mystery of the house appeared to the prophet, withal its priesthood, sacrifice, service, judgment, laws, statutes, and charge, besides every divine measurement. Finally the prophet returns to the mystical door of the house. 'I am the door.'

'Afterward he brought me again unto the door of the house; and, behold, waters issued out from under the threshold of the house eastward: for the forefront of the house stood toward the east, and the waters came down from under from the right side of the house, at the south side of the altar.

'Then brought he me out of the way of the gate northward, and led me about the way without unto the utter gate by the way that looketh eastward; and, behold, there ran out waters on the right side.

'And when the man that had the line in his hand went forth eastward, he measured a thousand cubits, and he brought me through the waters; the waters were to the ankles.

'Again he measured a thousand, and brought me through the waters; the waters were to the knees. Again he measured a thousand, and brought me through; the waters were to the loins.

'Afterward he measured a thousand; and it was a river that I could not pass over: for the waters were risen, waters to swim in, a river that could not be passed over.

'And he said unto me, Son of man, hast thou seen this? Then he brought me, and caused me to return to the brink of the river. Now when I had returned, behold, at the bank of the river were very many trees on the one side and on the other', Ezekiel 47:1-7.

From the fortieth chapter the prophet, having been transported in the Spirit from Babylon to the razed and overgrown foundations of Jerusalem and the temple, received revelation after revelation in the visions of God.

Spiritually his eyes were enlightened to behold the inconceivably mysterious appearance and dimensions of this spiritual house, measured by the man with the measuring reed. Vision upon vision appeared to Ezekiel, all filled with heavenly openings.

At last the prophet was brought back to the mystical door of the house. This is recorded at the beginning of the forty-seventh chapter.

Now Ezekiel is caused to behold waters issuing from under the threshold of the house eastward. That is, as ran the river out of Eden eastward to water the garden, so ran these waters from under the threshold of God's habitation, toward the east. 'For the forefront of the house stood toward the east.'

The mystical waters came down from under the right side of the house, that is, the side of the candlestick. Now the candlestick typified the *ecclesia*. This answered to the south side of the altar, and thence the waters flowed. For the altar is the place of sacrifice, the place of atonement, the place of substitutionary sacrifice, and thence rivers of blood flowed to make atonement for the sins of the people.

Then, blood and water flowed out at the south side, the candlestick side, and indicated the redemption of Christ made, accepted, and applied to his people and on their behalf. Thence, these waters flowed one way. And they flowed *only* one way. They flowed to the east. From the east, the Sun of righteousness should arise with healing in his beams.

This the prophet is caused to prove in his experience by the man with the measuring reed. 'Then brought he me out of the way of the gate'—of the courtyard wall which completely surrounded the house—'and led me about the way without unto the utter gate by the way that looketh eastward.'

The man led the prophet in the vision right around the house, till he returned to the place from which he began, namely, the east gate. Everywhere else was dry. But when he came to the east gate 'behold, there ran out waters on the right side.'

This was in line with the south side of the altar, whence there came not water only, but blood also, even the blood of one sacrifice for sins for ever in a figure. This in turn lined up with the candlestick—the *ecclesia* in the foreshadowing—the waters issuing forth from under the very foundation of God's habitation.

Thence the waters came. Through the gate, the east gate, they passed, flowing eastward.

Out towards the sunrising the man led the prophet through the water a thousand cubits—ten by ten by ten—ten threefold. Ten indicates completion; and three, divinity in the new covenant, that is, Father, Son, and Holy Ghost.

Here is a vision of the complete work of God. The waters flowed one way alone. *This* way. Thus far, to the ankles. Then, the walk was to be in the Spirit. The feet were to be washed. If so, baptized in one Spirit.

Again a thousand cubits. That is, ten threefold twice over. The waters came up to the knees. Not just the walk, the feet, but the knees also.

The knees present the first junction of the body to allow of vital progress, here perfectly wrought in God, baptized in the Holy Ghost, flowing all one way, from one source in one direction alone, and, at that, conducted by the man with the measuring line. Thus to walk, to run, to bend the knee: What could be more divine?

Again a thousand cubits. Ten threefold thrice over. Here is the fulness of God. Now God enlarges the stride of the prophet under him.

Borne along by the Holy Ghost, the waters were to the loins. Extended, comprehensive, strong movement, striding to the utmost, the waters submerging every joint of forward movement, as the prophet in vision surges from the hips with the flowing of the Holy Ghost to the fullest.

Once more a thousand cubits. But it was too much. The prophet could not pass over. Here were waters to swim in. Already these waters of the Spirit had caused the prophet experimentally in vision to answer to the measure of the stature of the fulness of Christ; for the measure of the river was the measure of a man: ankles; knees; loins; and, finally, out of depth above the head: waters to swim in.

But now, at the last, though breadth, length, depth, and height had been measured, there came that which passed knowledge. The prophet was out of his depth at such divine dimensions.

And is not this the river of God in a vision, a vision of the prophet between the foreshadowing in Eden, and the reality in heavenly Jerusalem? Does not Ezekiel's vision draw out the signification of the river that went forth eastward out of Eden? the spiritual waters from the smitten Rock, which Rock was Christ? and the river of God in the Psalms?

If not, what can these things signify? If not, what does this mean: 'Whosoever drinketh of this water'— whether of Eden; of the smitten rock; or of the Psalms; *this* water—'shall thirst again: but whosoever drinketh of the water that I shall give him *shall never thirst.'*

Then whatever kind of water is *that?* Where is it? How can one receive it? Whatever, *it is like no other water — however foretold or foreshadowed — like no other water the world has ever known, no, not since the foundation thereof.*

'But the water that I shall give him shall be in him a well of water springing up into everlasting life', John 4:13,14. Then this inwardly given water is not — as were all other waters; however spiritually significant — outwardly partaken, but inwardly outflowing.

For this water which Jesus gives is not natural water to quench bodily thirst, but spiritual water to slake soul drought. Here is *spiritual water* which *issues up from within the being unto everlasting life.* Then not only is this *living* water, but it is water which *causes to live for ever.* Of this, everything else about water was a mere figure.

Again he saith, 'He that believeth on me, as the scripture hath said, out of his belly shall flow rivers of living water. But this spake he of the Spirit, which they that believe on him should receive: for'—at that time—'the Holy Ghost was not yet given; because that Jesus was not yet glorified', John 7:38,39.

Now, here is more yet than the inward well-spring of living water, the water of everlasting life, welling up in the interior being, given by Jesus within. Here, all flows out: not one river, but as it were four heads, *rivers* of living water. And what is this if not better than paradise?

As to *this* water, 'Jesus stood and cried, saying, If any man thirst, let him come unto me, and drink', John 7:37. Since this drink is an inward well; since it springs out of the interior parts; since it multiplies in the issue; and since it is both living and everlasting, it must be spiritual.

And so he says 'This spake he of the Spirit'. Then, to come to him for it, must be to come to him spiritually. That is, within, in the inner man, from the heart. Again, it is to come to him as he is in reality, not as he is imagined to be in fantasy, or presumed to be in imagination, *but as he is in himself*. If so, as he is in the gospel, the evangel, the apostles' doctrine.

Then, everything is made clear. When *he* is seen, he shows his own things. 'And he showed me a pure river of water of life, clear as crystal, proceeding out of the throne of God and of the Lamb', Revelation 22:1. Mark that: *he* showed me. This is revelation; and it is interior revelation. There is nothing without this; and there is nothing of this without the gospel.

How could this river be seen by John? Because, as he said, '*he* showed me'. But how could John see it? Because he was shown it. But it is *spiritual*; it is *living*; it is *everlasting*. These things are invisible: how could John be shown them? By revelation alone. That is, by the revelation of Jesus Christ. This glorious revelation shines in the evangel.

This river, this pure river, this pure river of water of life, clear as crystal, proceeds out of the throne. This was seen in vision from Ezekiel: the waters issued from under the threshold of the house. It is well to perceive God's foundations.

This spiritual river conveys the blessing. The blessing is eternal life. The life of Father, Son, and Holy Ghost. These waters heal; they are pure, they cleanse; the tree of life is multiplied on the banks thereof, even everlasting life, the eternity of life. If so, this river springs to eternity.

'I Jesus have sent mine angel to testify unto you these things in all the churches. I am the root and the offspring of David, and the bright and morning star.

'And the Spirit and the bride say, Come. And let him that heareth say, Come. And let him that is athirst come. And whosoever will, let him take the water of life freely', Revelation 22:16,17.

He which testifieth these things saith, Surely I come quickly. Amen. Even so, come, Lord Jesus.

The grace of our Lord Jesus Christ be with you all. Amen.

V

The Two Trees in Eden

'AND out of the ground made the LORD God to grow every tree that is pleasant to the sight, and good for food; the tree of life also in the midst of the garden, and the tree of knowledge of good and evil', Genesis 2:9.

This verse introduces a new and strange element, quite different from anything which preceded.

'The tree of life also in the midst of the garden, and the tree of knowledge of good and evil.' Without comment—almost casually—this mystical allusion quietly slips into the flow of a narrative which, however spiritual its nature, remains otherwise solidly based on the tangible facts and actual occurrences of Creation.

The enigmatic reference to the two trees defies rational explanation. JEHOVAH Elohim had breathed into man's nostrils the breath of life. Why then a tree of life? Man's innocence depended upon his touching dependence upon the inbreathing of JEHOVAH Elohim maintaining his mind and soul: Why then a tree of knowledge?

And life for the soul from a tree? Or knowledge in the mind from fruit? These things are not compatible. If 'no man knoweth the things of God save by the Spirit of God'; and if 'no man knoweth the things of a man, save by the spirit of man which is in him', How can either divine or human things be conveyed by insensate vegetation?

The truth is that they cannot. Then why the mystery of the 'tree of life'? whence the enigma of 'the tree of knowledge'? What is the meaning of these things, elsewhere declared to be incompatible? For if divinity cannot be conveyed to humanity save by the divine Spirit; and if humanity cannot touch mankind save by the human spirit; What can *trees* do in the matter, which are utterly void of *any* spirit?

Then what do these things mean? Or, rather, how are they to be read? They *must* be regarded as symbols. They *must* be read symbolically. But the spiritual are fearful of symbolism in such a passage, for, once admit the principle, and the godless, by the time they have finished their plundering, will have Adam an emblem; Eve a token; the seven days a figure; and the word of God a fable.

But we ought not to proceed on a basis of the fear of our enemies, but upon that of the fear of God. The wicked flee when no man pursueth, and should such a man as I flee from the truth because of what these Philistines might do to it? For I have already pointed out what is plain, namely, that the names and descriptions of the two trees are unique in the narrative.

And if they are unique in the narrative, they require distinct principles of interpretation peculiar to them, not proper to the narrative itself. Symbols are obvious, and made doubly obvious by their separate character in the text. What applies to them, simply cannot apply to the rest of the text. We may safely trust the Spirit of God to make obvious his own choice of symbols, his own use of symbolism, and his own interpretation of symbolic figures, inappropriate to any other place.

So that before considering the tree of life, and the tree of knowledge of good and evil—so momentous, so awesome, so enduring in their significance — their names, their qualities, and their nature require one to ask, Are these *literal* trees at all? or are the literal qualities and nature of trees taken into the realm of symbolism, so as to utilize those properties as *figures* of spiritual realities?

Are the two trees, unique in their name and nature in the garden of Eden, chosen by the Holy Ghost—the more especially by the pen of Moses—to be representative of things in themselves intangible, invisible, and spiritual, but none the less real? Consider this.

Especially consider that trees are often used symbolically by the Holy Ghost to depict things to which superficially they bear no resemblance whatsoever, but, nevertheless, have *properties* which suggest the persons and things of which they are illustrative.

For example, Genesis 49:22, 'Joseph is a fruitful bough, even a fruitful bough by a well; whose branches run over the wall.' But Joseph was not a tree, nor had he branches. Nevertheless, symbolically the analogy was perfect. 'For the vineyard of the LORD of hosts is the house of Israel, and the men of Judah his pleasant plant', Isaiah 5:7. Yet neither the house of Israel, nor yet the men of Judah, bore the faintest *logical* resemblance to a vineyard or a plant. But they did symbolically.

Then is the assertion that I consider the tree of life and the tree of knowledge of good and evil to be symbolical, not literal, so strange that some suppose the next thing I shall dream up will be something like, 'I see men as trees, walking'? But that is precisely what was said in Mark 8:24. And what will my critics reply to this symbolism: 'The tree that thou sawest .... It is thou, O king', Daniel 4:20,22?

John the Baptist informed Israel of the cutting ministry of Christ, 'Now also the axe is laid unto the root of the trees', Matthew 3:10. Trees? Which trees? And in Matthew 13:32, the kingdom of heaven is likened unto a mustard tree. The kingdom of heaven a *tree*?

'For if thou wert cut out of the olive tree which is wild by nature, and wert graffed contrary to nature into a good olive tree: how much more shall these, which be the natural branches, be graffed into their own olive tree?', Romans 11:24. Where trees are beyond all reasonable doubt used symbolically by the Holy Ghost in holy scripture. And even used symbolically of Christ himself: 'I am the true vine', John 15:1.

Wherefore the symbolic use of trees is no novelty; nor is the proposition that the tree of life and the tree of knowledge of good and evil are symbols some flight of fancy. No scripture is of any private interpretation, and no title to fancy or opinion exists in any place or in the whole of the word of God. One must be led of the Spirit into the true and sole interpretation, or else confess one's ignorance and lay one's hand upon one's mouth in the fear of God in consequence.

True interpretation becomes obvious by the spiritual opening of the passage in and of itself. This is corroborated by the context, that is, the flow of the meaning both preceding and following the passage: the interpretation of the passage must agree with this flow.

Confirmation of this is obtained by the comparison of scripture with scripture, that there be no conflict, but rather that every scripture may be seen to harmonize with the scripture in question. And finally—and in a sense above all—the testimony of the Holy Ghost must be discerned in all and over all as bearing witness to the truth.

These are the principles to which I have been disciplined in the sight of God, bringing before you the proposition that the two trees in the garden of Eden—the tree of life and the tree of knowledge of good and evil—are symbolic. Having so said, I proceed to apply these principles to the opening of the meaning.

'And out of the ground made the LORD God to grow every tree that is pleasant to the sight, and good for food; the tree of life also in the midst of the garden, and the tree of knowledge of good and evil', Genesis 2:9. In context, consider the word 'every'. Observe: 'Out of the ground made the LORD God to grow *every* tree.'

This word is repeated in Genesis 2:16, 'Of *every* tree of the garden thou mayest freely eat.' The Hebrew *kol*, 'every', means precisely what it says: All; the whole; every; the complete number. That is, 'all' the trees. 'Every one' of the trees. The 'whole' of them: the 'complete number' of the trees, none excepted.

This is exemplified by the totality of the trees mentioned in Genesis 1:29. 'I have given you every herb bearing seed, which is upon the face of all the earth, *and every tree*, in the which is the fruit of a tree yielding seed; to you it shall be for meat.' These are called 'good', or 'very good', Genesis 1:31.

That is, Genesis 2:9, 'pleasant to the sight, and good for food.' This includes *every one* of the trees created and made. This is repeated over and over. No tree is excluded. *Every* tree is included. Not one tree in the garden is excepted. If 'every' does not mean that, what does it mean? And could it be more emphasized?

Now, if the word *kol* be not chosen, and reiterated in order to emphasize the totality of the trees formed by JEHOVAH Elohim, Why is it stated, reiterated, and emphasized? Why, if not to distinguish between *every*—literally created—tree, and *two* — symbolically figured — trees? What other reason could possibly exist for the repeated insertion of the word 'every' *when in fact two trees are excluded from that number?*

Pray, why else is 'every' inserted so particularly, and repeatedly, when otherwise it would be quite unnecessary? At the least it is evident, the word 'every' distinguishes between two classes: the one '*every* tree'; and the other 'the tree of life also, and the tree of knowledge of good and evil'. But for what purpose, save to illustrate that the trees as a whole are taken as an ideal figure of two essential but elusive spiritual verities?

'The tree of life also in the midst of the garden, and the tree of knowledge of good and evil', Genesis 2:9. Also? The tree of life *also*? But what does 'also' mean? for to convey that meaning, so that it *conditions* the text, this word is inserted by the Holy Ghost. Now I am aware that the Hebrew may be translated 'and'; but with no more force than 'also', and, quite rightly, the translators have given the latter rendering.

Ponder the word 'also'. This means 'as well as', or, 'in addition to'. But as well as what? In addition to what? Answer, As well as *'every'*. That is, In addition to *'every'*. Every what? Every *tree*. That is, in addition to *every* tree.

'Also' indicates that quite beside what had been mentioned before, the following was in existence. Namely, besides *every* tree, *also* there were two trees. But surely that contradicts the entire force of *'every'*?

If *every*, then nothing can be excluded. Yet despite the use, meaning, and force of the word *every*, the tree of life also, and the tree of knowledge of good and evil, *were* excluded. Then, in terms of trees, to make sense of the text, 'every' tree must have provided a picture of what *two symbolical trees represented*.

Take notice that besides 'every' tree, there were 'also' two trees, each of so peculiar and strange a description—beyond anything remotely connected with trees, or conceivably associated with vegetation—that beyond reasonable doubt this indicates a figure or analogy.

Since the inclusive term *every* embraces all trees distinguished by beauty and seed-bearing, being as it were cordoned off by the use of that word, it follows that by the use of the word 'also' the two strangely named trees outside of this cordon must refer to some unique sign.

Since 'also' refers to two mystically named symbols under the figure of 'trees', yet these are excluded from the number of every natural created tree, what is it but that the invisible, moral, and spiritual truths suggested by the nature of literal trees have been transposed to convey intangible and divine principles?

This alone accounts for Moses' desire to separate the tree of life and the tree of knowledge of good and evil from 'every' tree, yet by utilizing the word 'also', the suggestion of the *properties* of the trees in the garden is retained.

How can this dichotomy otherwise be reconciled than by the conclusion that whereas 'every' tree was literal, 'also' there were two spiritual principles symbolized as trees, the significance of which it is essential for the reader to grasp.

Many precedents exist in scripture for the particular use of trees in a purely symbolic form. For example, Psalm 1:3, 'He shall be like a tree'. Jeremiah 17:8, 'He shall be as a tree'. And, Numbers 24:6, Israel is symbolized 'as the trees of lign aloes which the LORD hath planted, and as cedar trees beside the waters.'

Ezekiel 31:3,5 informs the reader, 'Behold, the Assyrian was a cedar in Lebanon with fair branches, and with a shadowing shroud, and of an high stature; and his top was among the thick boughs. Therefore his height was exalted above all the trees of the field, and his boughs were multiplied, and his branches became long because of the multitude of waters, when he shot forth.'

Verses 7,8,9 continue, 'Thus was he fair in his greatness, in the length of his branches: for his root was by great waters.

The cedars in the garden of God could not hide him: the fir trees were not like his boughs, and the chestnut trees were not like his branches; nor any tree in the garden of God was like unto him in his beauty.

'I have made him fair by the multitude of his branches: so that all the trees of Eden, that were in the garden of God, envied him.' And now will anyone try to tell me that trees are not used by the Holy Ghost symbolically, and, at that, of or in the garden of Eden?

Again, Psalm 104:16, 'The trees of the LORD are full of sap; the cedars of Lebanon, which he hath planted.' Once more; they that mourn in Zion shall be called 'trees of righteousness, the planting of the LORD, that he might be glorified', Isaiah 61:3.

On the other hand presumptuous ungodly sinners, taking it upon themselves to speak—which the multitude of babblers in this present generation illustrates—are detested, being called 'trees whose fruit withereth, without fruit, twice dead, plucked up by the roots', Jude 12.

Leaving the general observation of trees symbolically used by the Holy Ghost, I come now to consider particularly the use of the tree of life in other places in the scriptures.

If—following the first occasion in Genesis—it can be proved that in *every other single reference* the use of the term tree of life is *never* literal, but *always* symbolical, sheer consistency in and of itself demonstrates that the same rule must hold good for the first occurrence of the term in Genesis 2:9 as it does for all following verses of the bible.

Let this once be established, and, beyond a peradventure, so strong an argument alone settles the question that the term 'tree of life' *never once refers to a literal tree, but always to a symbolic or figurative mystery.*

This alone settles the argument? But why should it be alone? I have before demonstrated by several conclusive proofs that the trees in the garden are figurative. Nor have I yet done with proofs ready marshalled to the same purpose. The consistent use of the tree of life in scripture as a symbol is certainly argument enough in itself. It may be more obvious but it is no less conclusive than any other reason submitted.

Proverbs 3:18 declares that the wisdom of God 'is a tree of life to them that lay hold upon her; and happy is every one that retaineth her.' Here the wisdom of God, which was from everlasting—and answers to the Word in the beginning—is said to be 'a tree of life'. But this wisdom, or Word, is not literally a tree of life. However, *figuratively* nothing describes such a spiritual reality more appropriately.

Again the wise man, teaching by the Holy Ghost, declares— Proverbs 11:30 —'The fruit of the righteous is a tree of life; and he that winneth souls is wise.' Here, first, the tree of life is a figure; it is a figure associated with the righteous; and the fruit of the righteous is like that of the figurative tree itself: it begets life. And so does the righteous man who winneth souls. Here is wisdom.

Proverbs 13:12 speaks of a bitter taste which experience has put in the mouths of many of the saints: 'Hope deferred maketh the heart sick.' So it does, and it seems to last for ever, without any mitigation or hope of fulfilment, 'How long wilt thou forget me, O Lord? for ever? how long wilt thou hide thy face from me? How long shall I take counsel in my soul, having sorrow in my heart daily?', Psalm 13:1,2.

Here is hope deferred, and the poor man hath the sickness in his heart, and the bile in his mouth, and, it seems, this goes on for ever. But hope cometh in the morning, and, turning from the darkness and gloom, the pain and affliction of legal chastisements, he sees the tree of life, and it is all over in a moment: 'But when the desire cometh, it is a tree of life', Proverbs 13:12.

Proverbs 15:4 states that a wholesome tongue is a tree of life: but perverseness therein is a breach in the spirit. A wholesome tongue will never take up an ill report against the neighbour; talebearing and malicious slander cannot be found there.

No; these are things from the serpent, and are as much a perpetual abomination to the LORD, as I have found the tongue of liars to fill evangelicalism with their perverseness, which, like a dead fish, stinks the nearer one comes to the head.

The wholesome tongue however is upright, and, being righteous, diffuses light, life, and love. This is by the gospel of Christ spoken in the Spirit. This is a tree of life.

But perverseness spoken in the flesh full of lies whispered to destroy the righteous, causes a breach in the Spirit. This grieves the Spirit world without end. The Holy Ghost is for ever with the righteous on one side of the breach, and to their everlasting shame evil speakers are on the other side of this great divide, the great gulf fixed, for ever void of the Spirit.

In these passages from the pen of the wise man, the son of David, we see that the tree of life is a proverb. That is, a parable. Or, as we say, symbolic. And the wise man takes up his parable and his sayings dark of old.

'I will incline mine ear to a parable: I will open my dark saying upon the harp.' 'I will open my mouth in a parable: I will utter dark sayings of old', Psalms 49:4 and 78:2. This agrees with Genesis 2:9. More: Jesus spake many things unto them in parables; and without a parable spake he not unto them. See Matthew 13:33-35.

'To him that overcometh'—and none other—saith the Spirit in the last book of the bible, 'will I give to eat of the tree of life, which is in the midst of the paradise of God', Revelation 2:7. But both paradise and tree were barred by a flaming sword.

And yet, both were quite destroyed and taken away at the Flood. How can this be? It could not be save that they were figures. Whence it follows, the place quoted from Genesis being in the book of Revelation, these things *must* have been figures.

Again, 'Blessed are they that do his commandments, that they may have right to the tree of life, and may enter in through the gates into the city', Revelation 22:14. As to these commandments, they are new testament commandments, namely, 'This is his commandment, That we should believe on the name of his Son Jesus Christ, and love one another, as he gave us commandment', I John 3:23.

'And he that keepeth his commandments dwelleth in him, and he in him. And hereby we know that he abideth in us, by the Spirit which he hath given us', I John 3:24. Now this is to eat of the tree of life, and to assimilate the fruit thereof, just as it is to enter into the gates of the city.

Of course this is couched in symbolic language. But then, so is the entire book of Revelation. For example, 'On either side of the river, was there the tree of life, which bare twelve manner of fruits, and yielded her fruit every month: and the leaves of the tree were for the healing of the nations. And there shall be no more curse', Revelation 22:2,3.

Now, we all know that the city; the river; the walls; the tree; the twelve manner of fruits; and so on, must of necessity be symbolic figures. For example, this is when time shall be no more; where they have no need of the sun or moon; for the Lord God Almighty and the Lamb are the light of the city. Then, months cannot apply. Ergo, 'Yielded her fruit every month' must be—like everything else—applied symbolically.

Blessed is the man in whom these symbols are realized; to whom these figures become realities; with whom these illustrations prove experimental. To lead to this very fulfilment such symbolism was set forth at the first, and reiterated at the last.

Through these graphic figures spiritual mysteries are depicted; invisible verities are given form; and intangible truths are made vivid. But the reality exceeds the symbol as high as the heavens are above the earth, just as the experience of the things symbolized passes all knowledge and every earthly sensation during this present life or in the world that now exists.

Now however I pass on to a further argument, which, given consideration, will prove invincible in and of itself. This demonstrates to a point that the trees in the garden are symbolical figures chosen by the Holy Ghost to represent things invisible and spiritual.

Consider: supposing the two trees were literal and not symbolic, given their immense importance, *the absence of any further mention of the tree of knowledge of good and evil in any other place in scripture after the second and third chapters of Genesis passes credulity.*

Observe that the tree of knowledge of good and evil is so prominent in the garden that it is intimately connected with the tree of life.

But if the tree of life is central to the truth 'in the midst of the garden'; if the tree of life appears in the first, last, and central book in scripture; then—the two trees being so closely connected—since the eating of the tree of knowledge of good and evil caused the Fall and brought in sin, death, and the curse: *How is it that after one brief mention that tree is never heard of again?*

How could this be? how is it conceivable? How is it possible that what brought the world, mankind, the age, and time itself into ruin — salvation from which occupies the entire word of God — should disappear without trace, unmentioned and unanswered? For it is certain that the tree of knowledge of good and evil never appears again after the Fall.

One brief reference, *then nothing*? It is not possible. Possible or not, it is nevertheless a fact that the tree of knowledge of good and evil simply passes into oblivion, never to be heard of again after Genesis chapters two and three.

Yet surely that is impossible. Impossible? But it is a fact. *Then the tree must have been a symbol, so that albeit the symbol never again receives a mention, nevertheless the thing symbolized occurs again and again till death be swallowed up in victory.* Only *then* will the Fall have been answered, for only *then* will the sentence 'In the day that thou eatest thereof thou shalt surely die' be seen to have found an antidote.

Yet that antidote *never appears against the name 'the tree of knowledge of good and evil'. Because that name never occurs again*. Then, it was a symbol, and so important a symbol, that the *thing symbolized immediately appears in its place throughout the remainder of old and new testament; of the whole scripture; of time itself; and of the revelation of the ways of God with man.*

There is no other explanation: the tree *must* have been symbolic. By such a token, it is *impossible* that it should have been literal.

What took place in the garden of Eden is in effect, however expressed, *the* major subject of the following volumes of holy scripture. Let any man ask himself, Is it possible that the tree of knowledge of good and evil should just *disappear* after one brief reference? No, it is not.

But then, it is not mentioned again. The answer, I repeat, the answer must be, it does not appear again in the symbolic form. But what the form symbolized is everywhere—must be everywhere—found in scripture.

The sum of what has been proposed teaches that the two specified trees in the garden of Eden are in fact symbolic. They are symbols to be used or discarded in scripture as seems good to the Holy Ghost. As it pleases God, the symbols may be retained or dismissed: but what can never change or be dismissed is the thing symbolized. This remains consistent from Genesis to Revelation.

The symbol of the tree of life reappears in Proverbs and Revelation. Hence at the first mention, however vaguely; in the second reference, no matter how poetically; and on the last occasion, no matter how dramatically: the tree of life is made manifest beyond the second and third chapters of Genesis. And yet entirely apart from such references, *the entire scriptures* are full of the *reality* of its symbolism.

In the case of the representation of the tree of knowledge of good and evil—the eating of which, in the figure, caused the Fall — this symbol never reappears. Nevertheless *the whole scripture* abounds with references to *the thing symbolized*.

Consider the prominence of this symbol in the garden, together with the omission of any further reference anywhere else in holy writ; combine this with the obvious fact that the entire scripture is full of the central truth that what was lost in Eden has been more than regained in Christ: What follows?

It follows by a law of necessity, that the tree of knowledge of good and evil—not to mention the tree of life—must be regarded as imagery, that is, a symbol to be interpreted spiritually.

One final argument, however, remains to be predicated in support of the proposition that the two specified 'trees'—outside of 'every' tree—in the garden of Eden are symbolic emblems depicted in the narrative to convey moral and spiritual verities. Namely, from the nature of trees, *it is impossible for these two trees to convey what their descriptive names suggest.*

Consider the scripture. 'The Spirit searcheth all things, yea, the deep things of God. For what man knoweth the things of a man, save the spirit of man which is in him? even so the things of God knoweth no man, but the Spirit of God', I Corinthians 2:10,11.

Here it is taught plainly that only the Spirit of God knows God's things, and only the spirit of man knows man's things. Whence it follows, without the gift of the Spirit, it is impossible for man to know the things of God.

If in divinity none but the divine can communicate divine things; if in humanity none but the human can partake of human things; how much less shall mere vegetation convey anything but perishable food? It is *impossible* for the two trees in the garden of Eden to convey to man what their names suggest.

Trees are arboreal. They are vegetation. They bear fruit. But neither the spirit of man nor human knowledge, bear any relation whatsoever to vegetation, trees, or fruit. There can be no connection in any way or at any time. These things belong to entirely separate realms having absolutely distinct properties which cannot be transposed.

No tree, no fruit of a tree—indeed, no food of any kind—can convey what is peculiar to man. 'For what man knoweth the things of a man, *save the spirit of man which is in him?*' The thing is impossible, whether it be of knowledge, or of any other human property. Trees, having no intelligent, moral, human life or being *can never communicate what they themselves do not possess, and cannot possess.*

This is just as clear from the reverse situation. Can man impart to a tree his own life, or endue vegetation with human knowledge?

Can man enable trees to think? Can a man transfer humanity to a tree, that it should have the qualities of mankind?

We have heard of a once blind man, his eyes being opened, saying that he saw men as trees walking. But whoso supposes to take this literally, one way or the other, is the opposite. Far from having his eyes opened, he is become as blind as a bat, and has no more brains than the trees of the wood.

What is material is conveyed by what is material. What is spiritual is imparted by what is spiritual. What is moral is vouchsafed by what is moral. Only divinity can bestow what is divine. And only humanity can communicate what is human.

These principles cannot be confused. They cannot be mixed. By a law of nature, the properties of the Creator, or of each distinct order of living Creation, cannot be transferred to another. It is beyond the realm of possibility that a tree should convey to man such things as the titles of the two trees in the garden propose. Therefore the trees are symbols, to be interpreted symbolically.

This leads immediately to the enquiry, What is the interpretation of the tree of life? And what is the hidden meaning of the tree of knowledge of good and evil? It is to these questions, and the respective answer and interpretation that belongs to the Spirit of God, that I address myself.

First it should be recalled what has been seen concerning the symbolic use of trees generally in the scriptures. Apart from the cedar representing the height and expanse of those who are great, the vast majority of such figures refer to uprightness or righteousness. Nor is the cedar exempt from this.

138

Consider the first psalm. 'Blessed is the man that walketh not in the counsel of the ungodly, nor standeth in the way of sinners, nor sitteth in the seat of the scornful. But his delight is in the law of the LORD; and in his law doth he meditate day and night.' Now, here is the righteous man, straight in his rejection of wickedness, and upright in his embracing of rectitude.

The psalm continues immediately, 'And he shall be like a tree planted by the rivers of water, that bringeth forth his fruit in his season; his leaf also shall not wither; and whatsoever he doeth shall prosper', Psalm 1:1-3. Here, root and branch, fruit and foliage, the tree symbolizes the upright man, the just or the righteous.

Likewise we have seen of Israel that he is fruitful and fragrant —as the lign aloes—upright and righteous—as the cedar. Once more, those who mourn in Zion are called 'trees of righteousness, the planting of the LORD, that he might be glorified', Isaiah 61:3. Now the LORD is justified in righteousness, and glorified in everlasting life. And this is the meaning.

It is because a tree by its very stature conveys uprightness, or righteousness, that Zion is spoken of in this manner. As to this rectitude, the justified in Zion conform, straight, true to the vertical, and upright. The fruit thereof is life in Zion, even eternal life, 'For there the LORD commanded the blessing, even life for evermore', Psalm 133:3. By this the LORD is glorified, because man has nothing to do with it, either with the righteousness or with the life.

Nor is the cedar, for all its loftiness, alone among the trees to be singled out by name in this respect. The palm tree also, notable for its straight and upright stature, is symbolic of righteousness. In Exodus 15:27 Israel came from the bitter waters of Marah, to the place Elim, where were twelve wells of water, and threescore and ten palm trees.

And does this speak of nothing but the bare fact? No: the bare fact speaks of everything for the spiritual blessing of Israel. Twelve wells could never be a mere coincidence, any more than seventy palm trees.

Twelve speaks of covenant Israel, indicative of the twelve tribes. Whereas waters of the well are figurative of the Holy Ghost springing up into everlasting life, and seven—which is perfection — times ten — which is completeness — tells of the perfection of the righteousness of faith brought in by the completed, or finished work of Christ for the unconditional justification of his covenant people.

In Psalm 92:12,13 we are informed that 'the righteous shall flourish like the palm tree: he shall grow like a cedar in Lebanon. Those that be planted in the house of the Lord shall flourish in the courts of our God.' Here the righteous are compared to a palm tree and a cedar. God planted them, their righteousness is from him, and so is the sap of life rising up from the root of Jesse.

Likewise Song 7:7, 'This thy stature is like to a palm tree.' And again, Judges 4:5, Deborah, a prophetess, judged Israel: 'She dwelt under the palm tree of Deborah between Ramah and Bethel'; and although she did so literally, yet what was literal was also a figure.

Now a palm tree speaks of the righteousness of faith, and if *her own* palm tree, then of *her* justification in righteousness. Ramah means 'high place', and Bethel, 'the house of God', that is, of the *living* God. And what is this but righteousness and life? For 'the fruit of the righteous is a tree of life', Proverbs 11:30.

Whence it appears that the tree itself is a symbol of righteousness. Nevertheless in the garden of Eden this is not the aspect that is stressed. Rather the *fruit* of the tree is the emphasis at the Creation. Genesis 1:12, 'The tree yielding fruit, whose seed was in itself.' Once more, Genesis 1:29, 'every tree, in the which is the fruit of a tree yielding seed; to you it shall be for meat.'

Again, Genesis 2:9, 'Out of the ground made the LORD God to grow every tree that is pleasant to the sight, and good for food.' The food provided by every tree—and, of course, herb— answered to nourishment for the body. The herb and the tree were given to man in the garden for meat.

This natural food was provided so that man's physical life should be sustained. The pleasantness to the sight of the upright trunk was not the emphasis here, but rather the boughs hanging heavy with fruit. This fruit was the food which nourished and sustained the body.

In a word, bodily life. As to the soul, the life of the soul was from the breath of God: 'And the LORD God formed man of the dust of the ground'—this physical formation was to be maintained by food from both herb and tree—'and breathed into his nostrils the breath of life; and man became a living soul'—this life of the soul was to be sustained by the breath of the LORD God.

Thus man was nourished and kept in innocence. But a light shone, and shone forth concerning a future purpose. And, John 1:4, 'The life'—mark that, *the life*—'was the light of men.' Man received the life of his soul from the inbreathing of the LORD God: but this—that is, the life that was the light of men— *was far more than that inbreathing*, and of this, Adam never partook.

The text reads in full, 'In him was life; and the life was the light of men', John 1:4. In Adam was a kind of life, *but it was not the kind of life which is called 'the light of men'*. The light *radiating from that life* was that which illuminated the life breathed into the living soul of Adam, but *it was distinct from it*.

141

The life was not the *life* of men. The life was the *light* of men. The living soul of Adam had a light cast upon it, and this light *came from another life, another kind of life, than that with which he had been created.* Because the light came from a life which had never been created.

'In him was life.' Not in Adam. In *him.* That is, in the Word. As yet unknown, though promised; unrevealed, yet dwelling with the Father and with the Holy Ghost, one God, blessed for evermore.

The light of life showed that the *ultimate* destiny of man was to live by him. Yet this could not be fulfilled until he was made manifest in the fulness of time. Nevertheless light shone forth on the truth of the uncreated, divine, everlasting life of the Son, just as veiled prophecy surely promised his coming. And this was the light of men.

'In the beginning was the Word, and the Word was with God, and the Word was God. The same was in the beginning with God. All things were made by him; and without him was not anything made that was made. In *him* was life; and the life was the *light* of men', John 1:1-4.

The living soul of natural man in the present Creation never could and never did fulfil the end of God's purpose for humanity. Nevertheless a light shone forth upon and from that purpose. But despite this light man turned to darkness, the Fall came in, sin and death reigned, and the curse sounded.

'And the light shineth in darkness; and the darkness comprehended it not', John 1:5. But in the fulness of time 'the life was manifested'—not the light: that had shined in the garden; at and after the Fall; despite the darkness; it shone forth in the darkness even from ages and from generations till —'the life was manifested, and we have seen it'.

The apostles saw, and John writes, 'For the life was manifested, and we have seen it, and bear witness, and show unto you that eternal life, which was with the Father'—from eternity; promised at Creation—'and was manifested unto us', I Jn. 1:2.

From the foundation of the earth, from the Creation of the world, from the beginning of time, this is the light that illuminated man: 'In him was life; and the life was the light of men.' Symbolically, this was set forth under the figure of the tree of life, shining upon and illuminating Adam as to the purpose of God yet to be fulfilled.

'The tree of life also in the midst of the garden, and the tree of knowledge of good and evil.'

I come now in particular to consider the tree of life in the midst of the garden of Eden.

It is evident that—however illuminated he may have been by the truth set forth in the figure—Adam never ate of this tree. This was set forth 'in the midst of the garden'. But the tree of knowledge of good and evil was not in the midst of the garden.

The wording is, And out of the ground made the Lord God to grow every tree that is pleasant to the sight, and good for food: 'The tree of life also in the midst of the garden'. Then, 'and'—meaning, as well as the tree in the midst, but apart from it—'the tree of knowledge of good and evil'.

Eve, when tempted by the figure of the serpent, professed, 'We may eat of the fruit of the trees of the garden: but of the fruit of *the tree which is in the midst of the garden*, God hath said, Ye shall not eat of it, neither shall ye touch it, lest ye die', Genesis 3:2,3.

Here are three lies. First, *the* tree which was in the *midst* of the garden was the tree of life. 'The tree of life also in the midst of the garden', Genesis 2:9. That precise wording was not used of the forbidden tree. Wherefore Eve misrepresented the forbidden tree to be the tree of life, the tree which was actually in the midst, which, evidently, she had not touched, or her wording would not have been applicable.

Eve lied when she said God had forbidden man the tree—which was the tree of life—in the midst of the garden. She transferred the names. But, even as she misrepresented the names of the trees, she also showed that she had not eaten of the tree of life.

Eve lied again when she said God had forbidden them to touch it. God had said no such thing. God forbad them to *eat* of the *other* tree than that which was in the midst. Touching was not forbidden in either case.

Finally, Eve lied when, having uttered two falsehoods, she affirmed that should they eat, or touch, the forbidden tree, God had said, *'lest'*— that is, in case —'ye die'.

What God said was this: 'Of every tree of the garden thou mayest freely eat: but of the tree of the knowledge of good and evil'—no *midst* of the garden here—'thou shalt not eat of it:'—no *neither shall ye touch it* here—'for in the day that thou eatest thereof *thou shalt surely die*', Genesis 2:16,17. No *lest* ye die here.

Then, man had not eaten, and neither did he ever eat, no, not even in innocence, of the fruit of the tree which was in the midst of the garden. That tree, by definition, was the tree of life. Albeit figures are used, nevertheless the figures *furnish abundant proof of the events of which they are figurative.*

As to eating of the tree of life *after* the Fall, this never happened, nor could it happen. Of Adam and his fallen posterity, which is of the flesh, and answers to the seed of the serpent, the LORD God spake on this wise:

'Behold, the man is become as one of us, to know good and evil: and now, *lest he put forth his hand, and take also of the tree of life, and eat,* and live for ever: Therefore the LORD God sent him forth from the garden of Eden, to till the ground from whence he was taken.

'So he drove out the man; and he placed at the east of the garden of Eden Cherubims, *and a flaming sword which turned every way, to keep the way of the tree of life*', Genesis 3:22-24. Here it is obvious, first, that man never took and ate of the tree of life in innocence, and, second, lest he should do so in guilt, he was driven out of the garden, his return being made impossible.

If so, none that are born of the flesh, called the seed of the serpent, eat anything in religion but the tree of the knowledge of good and evil. However it is equally obvious that a hidden mystery, a wholly distinct seed chosen in Christ before the foundation of the world, *do* find access to the tree of life, the sword of justice having been sheathed in the side of Christ, and, by the righteousness of faith, these eat, and live for ever.

What did Moses mean by the 'tree of life', weaving this figure or symbol of divine and spiritual concept into the rich tapestry of the reality of Creation, of Adam, of Eve, and of the garden of Eden? It has been shown to a demonstration that this is a symbol; but of what is it a symbol?

From the proven symbolic use of trees throughout the scripture, it has been demonstrated that trees as such signify uprightness or righteousness. This follows from their very nature. It stands out in beholding their stature: trees of righteousness shall the LORD call them; 'upright as the palm tree'.

But in this case it is not the tree, but what it bears that gives it the distinctive name 'tree of *life*'. Evidently, that is what it bears. The fruit, rather than the tree which bears it, is the

145

cause of its name: Life. But I have before shown, not the life of a human soul, namely, mortal life, breathed into man's nostrils. And if not, then the life that is divine, the life of him 'who only hath immortality', that is, eternal life.

For the *life* was manifested—which *then* had been the light of men—that life which was with the Father—*then*, but unknown as such, because the deity was not *then* revealed, save as ELOHIM in Creation, and JEHOVAH Elohim to Israel — 'the life was manifested, which was with the Father, and was manifested unto us'. If so, at the coming of the Son into the world.

At Creation, the light shone forth from the Word, but not so as to reveal who he was in person, who shone so brightly with such radiant beams. He was not made manifest in the glory of his Sonship, nor was it revealed that there were three divine Persons in one God, and one God in three divine Persons. That revelation awaited the coming of the new testament.

The Word of life, the *tree* of life, mystically set forth God's eternal purpose, hidden from the foundation of the world, but promised at his coming. What should then be manifested was the life of the Son of God. 'For the life was manifested, and we have seen it', I Jn. 1:2. This is the true God, and eternal life.

This life, this eternal life, symbolized as God's ultimate purpose for humanity, never realized in innocence—for so soon man transgressed—was to come by way of righteousness. That is, despite the Fall, despite sin, despite the outraged justice of God, God would find a way of atonement, by which he would bring to pass the promise of eternal life by Jesus Christ.

Being justified freely by his grace through the redemption that is in Christ Jesus, it is *he* 'whom God hath set forth to be a propitiation through faith in his blood, to declare his right-eousness for the remission of sins that are past, through the forbearance of God', Romans 3:24,25.

That remission, through 'the Lamb slain from the foundation of the world'—that is, in the counsels of God, Revelation 13:8— that remission, I say, and its consequent free justification, in which the righteousness of God is accounted to the ungodly, reaches back in its effectiveness from Golgotha to Eden.

It was for 'the remission of sins that are past'. That is, the sins of the elect from the foundation of the world up to the death of the Son. But not only so: 'To declare, I say, at this time'—the time of Paul's writing; from that time henceforth; through history to this time; today—'at *this* time *his* righteousness: that he might be just, and the justifier of him which believeth in Jesus', Romans 3:26.

For by the blood of Christ, shed to appease God's wrath, both under the law, and in his own nature, the righteousness of God is vindicated in his justly forgiving sinners. Christ has paid the price, and righteousness is freely imputed without works. This is seen in the tree itself in a figure.

'Christ hath redeemed us from the curse of the law, being made a curse for us: for it is written, Cursed is every one that hangeth on a tree', Galatians 3:13. 'Who his own self bare our sins in his own body on the tree', I Pet. 2:24.

'And when Israel came to Marah'—near dying of thirst—'they could not drink of the waters of Marah, for they were bitter: therefore the name of it was called Marah. And the people murmured against Moses, saying, What shall we drink? And he cried unto the LORD; and the LORD showed him a tree, which when he had cast into the waters, the waters were made sweet', Exodus 15:23-25.

Whence you see in a figure, that there is no obtaining life, or the water of life, or the fruit of life, till righteousness is vindicated, and judgment passed—as one might so speak—on the tree. This was cut down, life for life, or the waters gave life to others.

In the reality, not the tree, but the life of him who hung upon it vicariously in suffering and death, was the vindication of God's justice in forgiving those for whom Christ died.

Life was promised in Eden to Adam in innocence, life transcending all that man could conceive. Now, this was set forth in the figure of a tree. If so, it would come by way of righteousness. That is, 'the fruit of the righteous'— of the justified, namely, the justified by faith—'is a tree of life', and that life is everlasting life through faith in his name.

And this is the heart of the gospel. 'I am not ashamed of the gospel of Christ ... for therein is the righteousness of God revealed', see Romans 1:16,17. Even as it is written, Romans 5:21, 'That as sin hath reigned unto death, even so might grace *reign through righteousness*'—there is the tree—'*unto eternal life* by Jesus Christ our Lord.' And here is the fruitfulness of the life.

Even as the apostle says in another place, Romans 8:10, 'The Spirit is life *because of righteousness*'. This is the tree of life, not in a figure, but in the reality. Righteousness and life are inexorably connected. There can be no life without righteousness. Now, the tree of life depicts the righteousness of God by faith of Jesus Christ, and if so, bears the fruit of everlasting life.

This blessed and everlasting life comes by the righteousness of faith. 'Even as David also describeth the blessedness of the man, unto whom God imputeth righteousness without works', Romans 4:6. That is, God wrought out a free, divine righteousness by the blood and in the death of Jesus Christ, unto all and upon all them that believe.

Being divine righteousness, it must be an everlasting righteousness that is freely reckoned to every one that believeth in Jesus. But if it be everlasting righteousness, such a tree can bear no less a fruit than eternal life. *This* is the tree of life.

But there were *two* trees in the garden. It must be so, there cannot be *one*, because there is *another* way of righteousness, just as there was, and is, another kind of life. No one was better or more experimentally acquainted with this truth than Moses, and, revealing that truth under the name JEHOVAH Elohim—the covenant name exclusive to Israel—it follows of necessity that this also should be set forth in a figure.

This *other* figure, symbolically the tree of knowledge of good and evil, occurs in parallel with the tree of life. 'The tree of life also in the midst of the garden, and the tree of knowledge of good and evil', Genesis 2:9.

Now, what does the tree of knowledge of good and evil represent? Whatever, by this symbol JEHOVAH Elohim warned, saying, 'Of every tree of the garden thou mayest freely eat: but of the tree of the knowledge of good and evil, thou shalt not eat of it: for in the day that thou eatest thereof thou shalt surely die', Genesis 2:16,17.

Why was this? Was the tree bad in itself, or was the fruit thereof—laughably depicted by fools as an 'apple'—evil? Evil? What nonsense is this? It is clerical, traditional, theological nonsense, not fit for the dustbin. How can *knowledge* be evil? How can the knowledge *of good* be evil? How can—not the *doing*, but to avoid the doing—the *knowledge* of evil be evil?

If it were evil, how was it that JEHOVAH Elohim said, 'Behold, *the man is become as one of us*'—now, who dares say the tree of the knowledge of good and evil was evil?—'become', saith the LORD God, 'as one of us, *to know good and evil*', Genesis 3:22. So what is this nonsense that the knowledge of good and evil was *intrinsically evil*? It was not.

What it was in fact appeared in JEHOVAH Elohim's admonition: It was *deadly dangerous and utterly unsuited to the appetite of man*. But that does not make it evil in itself. It makes it folly to man, and, after the commandment of the LORD God, it makes it disobedience for man, to take and eat of it.

By definition, the tree of *knowledge* of good and evil could not be bad in itself. It was bad *for man*. Man *must never* attempt to sustain life before God in such a way, no matter how attractive—pleasant to the eyes—it appeared: JEHOVAH Elohim had not prohibited it for nothing.

Silly ignorance—and unspiritual, uninspired interpretations —concerning the figure of the serpent, and the awareness of nakedness after the Fall, do more to manifest the blindness of superstition and the uncleanness of fallen mentality, than they do to cast light on the mysterious and veiled truth of the tree of the knowledge of good and evil.

Adam was in innocence: that is, a simple, trusting, and childlike dependence on the divine inbreathing to keep and sustain the life of his soul. Man in innocence dwelt in and lived by that breath of life: he had neither thought nor need of any other support. The promise of eternal life at a coming revelation in the fulness of time, though Adam was aware of it, altered nothing *of his present life of and in innocence.*

Innocent of good and evil, aware only of dependence on the breath of and life inbreathed from JEHOVAH Elohim: here was all his guidance. That life led him, and by it he lived. The tree of knowledge of good and evil was *per se* unnecessary to that innocent life. Moreover, it was *deadly* to it.

Deadly to it, because to live by the knowledge of good and evil was to *depart from living upon, in, and by the inbreathing of the breath of life in which he had been created.*

For the symbolic tree presupposed two things. One, that man *needed* knowledge, and was capable of assimilating it, in order to live rightly. Two, that man, given that knowledge, *had the strength and ability in himself* to live by the understanding he would have gained by the assimilation of that knowledge.

But that supposition would deny the very nature of what he had been created to be in innocence. It would deny his humanity, sustained by inbreathing from Jehovah Elohim. It would be to transfer that dependence to the assumption of an ability to live independently of the breath of Jehovah Elohim, relying upon his own knowledge and his own ability.

It would be to fly in the face of the warning of the Lord God. It would be to bring down instant death by turning from the source of his life, to suppose that he could live without that source, substituting for it what subsisted independently within himself. It would be to defy the Lord God, and rebel against his express commandment.

What did the symbol of the tree of the knowledge of good and evil represent?

The interpretation discovered throughout scripture concerning the figurative use of trees—a figure seen to be applicable to the tree of life—applies equally to the tree of the knowledge of good and evil. Looked at in terms of figurative interpretation the application must be consistent. It must apply to this tree also. Then, the tree itself represents righteousness.

But not the same righteousness. Another righteousness. For there *are* two standards of righteousness, and two ways of righteousness, from one end of the bible to the other. And two only.

The first has been shown to signify the righteousness of faith, that is, the righteousness of God by faith of Jesus Christ. This righteousness of God, divinely wrought by the Father and the Son, is imputed to faith.

However there is another way of righteousness, and there is only one other way of righteousness: it is the righteousness of the law. This must be attained by works commensurate and consistent with its standard.

Such a legal standard *gives* no righteousness; rather, it gives the knowledge of righteousness, commanding good and prohibiting evil. It is therefore the knowledge of good and evil, and requires works equal to the rectitude which it describes.

But the law must be set forth and revealed variously in commandments, ordinances, judgments, precepts, and words. This demands knowledge, and presupposes a mentality equal to its doctrine. In turn, this requires judgment, presupposing the ability to choose the good and eschew the evil. Finally, this presumes strength and power in man equal to keeping the commandment. That is the righteousness of the law.

And if such solemn matters can better be figured than by the symbol of the tree of the knowledge of good and evil, I should like to know how. For the truth is, *thus* the Holy Ghost set forth *the only other way of righteousness*, that is, the righteousness of the law, by this very figure.

Here is symbolized the only other way of attaining righteousness, that is, the righteousness demanded by the law. This is not by faith, the law requires no faith, but it is by works, for the law demands works, as it is written, The man that doeth them shall live by them. But that no man is justified by the works of the law is evident, for, The just shall live by faith.

What! Man the mental ability to assimilate the law? What! Man the judgment to discern between good and evil? What! Man the ability to keep the commandments? Hear the word of the LORD: 'Therefore by the deeds of the law there shall no flesh be justified in his sight: for by the law is the knowledge of sin', Romans 3:20.

Knowledge? 'Full well ye reject the commandment of God, that ye may keep your own tradition', Mark 7:9. Judgment? 'Ye judge after the flesh', John 8:15. Ability? 'Who have received the law by the disposition of angels, and have not kept it', Acts 7:53. But long ago, and far away, all this was foreseen in a symbol. But man *would* eat of it, for he *will* make much of himself in religion.

Since the law gives no life, but only knowledge, and since the works of the law give no life, but must be kept—and kept continually—to earn it, no life will ever be attained from this quarter, as it is written, 'In the day that thou eatest thereof thou shalt surely die', Genesis 2:17.

Therefore, dimly, in the most veiled symbol — as was the tree of life—yet in essential principle, the tree of knowledge of good and evil set forth the righteousness of the law, or, in a word, the concept of works. However the legal principle can do no more than convey the knowledge of how to attain to its righteousness, in fact presupposing what is not in man's nature to render.

It is not that the law is not spiritual, but Adam was innocent, and all his desire was for the inbreathing which gave him being. Till he fell. After the Fall, the law abode spiritual. 'For we know that the law is spiritual: but I am carnal'—says Paul, Romans 7:14—'sold under sin.' And it was Adam that did the selling, on behalf of his entire posterity.

It is not that the law is not holy, just, and good. But man in innocence needed no such rule. But, innocence lost, in the Fall, 'Was then that which is good made death unto me? God forbid. But sin, that it might appear sin, working death in me by that which is good', Romans 7:13.

It was not in man in innocence, and it is not in man in the Fall, to find anything in the righteousness of the law save the exceeding sinfulness of sin, and the unalterable cursing of death.

'Now we know that what things soever the law saith, it saith to them who are under the law: that every mouth may be stopped, and all the world may become guilty before God', Romans 3:19.

Thus far to draw to a close. The Man of promise alluded to by ELOHIM in Genesis 1:26,27, is the embodiment of the tree of life, and is to his people, that chosen seed, both righteousness and life in and of himself. This is one thing.

Here is another thing, for two things pertain to this matter. The man who lost his innocence, and never partook of the tree of life, was he who disobeyed. Adam transgressed, he fell, and ate of the tree whereof JEHOVAH Elohim commanded him that he should not eat. This is the man of Genesis 2:7, the earthy man, the man of sin and death. To him and to his seed pertains the tree of the knowledge of good and evil.

He would be independent of the inbreathing of God. He would puff up his fleshly mind with knowledge he was incapable of realizing or utilizing. He would exalt himself by dependency on his own judgment. He would swell with pride as if he had life, strength, or power to keep the righteousness by which he proposed to live before God.

And this to please God? For it is not a question of licentiousness, or vileness, but of *righteousness*. But a righteousness which in its effect puffs up the fleshly mind, exalts human judgment, and swells the pride of the man who *will* do things for God, and who *cannot* submit to God doing things for him.

Thus the works of the law become that man: the righteousness of the law is his choice. But he says, and does not. He cannot and he will not attain to what he professes: for by the law is the knowledge of sin.

Someone may object, But the law was given by Moses: this was so long after Eden: How then could the tree symbolize the righteousness of the law?

First, I answer, And grace and truth came by Jesus Christ: this was vastly later than the law: Why then did you not object when it was shown that the tree of life was a veiled, mysterious symbol of that eternal life which came ages and generations after Moses?

This objection springs from ignorance of the law. Certainly as a formal covenant, *a system of justification*, the declaration of the righteousness of the law was given by Moses.

But just as the exposition of that law could not be reduced to a few commandments, which was expanded to virtually two and a half volumes—in Exodus; Leviticus; and Deuteronomy— so the two and a half volumes *still* do not express the *entirety* of the law.

It was not that the essential principle of law was not *there* between Adam and Moses. But it was not expressed; it was not divinely expressed; it was not expressed as a system of justification; and it was not expressed as a covenant enjoined by Jehovah with Israel. In *that* sense, the law came by Moses.

But as an unspoken moral concept the essence of the law was there. It must have been there. Law was not, and is not, invented; it cannot mutate or alter: it is inexorable, universal, immutable, and absolute. This *concept* stood from the creation of man.

Because the law stands on moral principles; it is based in moral relations. That is why I say it was not invented. Given moral relationships, *law is; it exists in virtue of those relationships.* Hence the tree was there.

The tree, symbolically, was there because with the creation of man *of necessity a moral relationship existed between him and his Creator.* This moral existence formed the foundation of moral obligation. The same is true of men. Given the increase of humanity *a moral relationship exists between men of necessity.* This necessity forms the basis of moral obligation.

Hence, given the creation of man, law follows of course *in its essence.* Hence the tree of the knowledge of good and evil was *there* because that moral being, or living soul, *existed.* But that did not mean that he should eat of the tree or think to live by it.

That law in essence was there, appears in Paul's comment on the Gentiles, who never received the law: 'which show the work of the law written in their hearts, their conscience also bearing witness', Romans 2:15. Not the *law* written in their hearts, mark: that would have been express. But *the work* of the law written in their hearts.

Of course it was. Moral relationships create moral obligations, and a moral, living soul cannot be without the weight of obligation within himself which such morality demands. No covenant; no legal system of justification; no expression: yes, but every obligation.

The ten commandments are not the essence of this. They are ten facets of it, created by shining the light, as upon a diamond, to reflect on that facet facing any one of ten obligations. But the ten facets are not the diamond. They are the facets of the diamond.

The one essence — call it the diamond — is the essential principle of law. With full light, expanded, expressed, covenanted, enjoined, it is a system of righteousness for justification. Self-justification. And man should never eat of it; he can never live by it; he can only die by it.

What man needed till the coming of Christ was what Adam lost: innocence. But that was what he lost because he *would* have his own righteousness for God. But God had his own righteousness for man. And that is what the tree of life set forth in the beginning.

'But Israel, which followed after the law of righteousness'— no wonder Moses wrote these mysteries of Israel's ultimate origin under the covenant name of JEHOVAH—'hath not attained to the law of righteousness.

'Wherefore? Because they sought it not by faith, but as it were by the works of the law. For they stumbled at that stumblingstone.'

'For they being ignorant of God's righteousness, and going about to establish their own righteousness, have not submitted themselves unto the righteousness of God.'

Two trees; two ways of righteousness; two men; two seeds. These things can never cross, nor be crossed.

Adam and his seed are for ever barred by JEHOVAH Elohim from the tree of life by a flaming sword turning every way. Christ and his seed find the sword sheathed in the side of the Saviour, and, from the tomb, in the resurrection, are for ever dead to the tree of the knowledge of good and evil.

If it be by grace, it is no more works: otherwise grace is no more grace; but if it be of works, it is no more grace: otherwise work is no more work, Romans 11:6.

Now nothing could more perfectly express the matter: two trees; two ways of righteousness; two men; two seeds. And these things can never be crossed. Otherwise the character of both is not only obscured beyond sight: it is lost beyond recovery.

This is so plainly set forth by the symbols of the tree of life, and the tree of the knowledge of good and evil.

One gives life, the other knowledge; one grants righteousness, the other requires righteousness; one bestows the righteousness of God, the other demands righteousness from man; one justifies unto eternal life, the other condemns to everlasting death.

One is free, the other is earned; one is given, the other is sought; one is of grace, the other of law; one is by faith, the other is of works; one gives peace, the other works wrath; and whilst the one makes men to boast, the other gives all the glory to God.

'For Christ is *the end of the law* for righteousness to every one that believeth', Romans 10:4. Thanks be unto God for his unspeakable gift. Amen, and Amen.

JOHN METCALFE

INDEX

TO OTHER PUBLICATIONS

i

PSALMS, HYMNS AND SPIRITUAL SONGS

THE PSALMS

OF THE

OLD TESTAMENT

The Psalms of the Old Testament, the result of years of painstaking labour, is an original translation into verse from the Authorised Version, which seeks to present the Psalms in the purest scriptural form possible for singing. Here, for the first time, divine names are rendered as and when they occur in the scripture, the distinction between LORD and Lord has been preserved, and every essential point of doctrine and experience appears with unique perception and fidelity.

The Psalms of the Old Testament is the first part of a trilogy written by John Metcalfe, the second part of which is entitled *Spiritual Songs from the Gospels*, and the last, *The Hymns of the New Testament*. These titles provide unique and accurate metrical versions of passages from the psalms, the gospels and the new testament epistles respectively, and are intended to be used together in the worship of God.

Price £2.50 *(postage extra)*
(hard-case binding, dust-jacket)
Printed, sewn and bound
by the John Metcalfe Publishing Trust
ISBN 0 9506366 7 3

SPIRITUAL SONGS

FROM

THE GOSPELS

The *Spiritual Songs from the Gospels*, the result of years of painstaking labour, is an original translation into verse from the Authorised Version, which seeks to present essential parts of the gospels in the purest scriptural form possible for singing. The careful selection from Matthew, Mark, Luke and John, set forth in metrical verse of the highest integrity, enables the singer to sing 'the word of Christ' as if from the scripture itself, 'richly and in all wisdom'; and, above all, in a way that facilitates worship in song of unprecedented fidelity.

The *Spiritual Songs from the Gospels* is the central part of a trilogy written by John Metcalfe, the first part of which is entitled *The Psalms of the Old Testament*, and the last, *The Hymns of the New Testament*. These titles provide unique and accurate metrical versions of passages from the psalms, the gospels and the new testament epistles respectively, and are intended to be used together in the worship of God.

Price £2.50 *(postage extra)*
(hard-case binding, dust-jacket)
Printed, sewn and bound
by the John Metcalfe Publishing Trust
ISBN 0 9506366 8 1

THE HYMNS

OF THE

NEW TESTAMENT

The *Hymns of the New Testament*, the result of years of painstaking labour, is an original translation into verse from the Authorised Version, which presents essential parts of the new testament epistles in the purest scriptural form possible for singing. The careful selection from the book of Acts to that of Revelation, set forth in metrical verse of the highest integrity, enables the singer to sing 'the word of Christ' as if from the scripture itself, 'richly and in all wisdom'; and, above all, in a way that facilitates worship in song of unprecedented fidelity.

The *Hymns of the New Testament* is the last part of a trilogy written by John Metcalfe, the first part of which is entitled *The Psalms of the Old Testament*, and the next, *Spiritual Songs from the Gospels*. These titles provide unique and accurate metrical versions of passages from the psalms, the gospels and the new testament epistles respectively, and are intended to be used together in the worship of God.

Price £2.50 *(postage extra)*
(hard-case binding, dust-jacket)
Printed, sewn and bound
by the John Metcalfe Publishing Trust
ISBN 0 9506366 9 X

'THE APOSTOLIC FOUNDATION OF THE CHRISTIAN CHURCH' SERIES

Third Printing

FOUNDATIONS UNCOVERED

THE APOSTOLIC FOUNDATION
OF THE
CHRISTIAN CHURCH

Volume I

Foundations Uncovered is the introduction to the major series: 'The Apostolic Foundation of the Christian Church'.

Rich in truth, the Introduction deals comprehensively with the foundation of the apostolic faith under the descriptive titles: The Word, The Doctrine, The Truth, The Gospel, The Faith, The New Testament, and The Foundation.

The contents of the book reveal: The Fact of the Foundation; The Foundation Uncovered; What the Foundation is not; How the Foundation is Described; and, Being Built upon the Foundation.

'This book comes with the freshness of a new Reformation.'

Price 75p *(postage extra)*
(Laminated cover)
Printed, sewn and bound
by the John Metcalfe Publishing Trust
ISBN 0 9506366 5 7

Thoroughly revised and extensively rewritten
second edition

Third Printing

THE BIRTH OF JESUS CHRIST

THE APOSTOLIC FOUNDATION
OF THE
CHRISTIAN CHURCH

Volume II

'The very spirit of adoration and worship rings through the pages of *The Birth of Jesus Christ.*

'The author expresses with great clarity the truths revealed to him in his study of holy scriptures at depth. We are presented here with a totally lofty view of the Incarnation.

'John Metcalfe is to be classed amongst the foremost expositors of our age; and his writings have about them that quality of timelessness that makes me sure they will one day take their place among the heritage of truly great Christian works.'

From a review by Rev. David Catterson.

'Uncompromisingly faithful to scripture ... has much to offer which is worth serious consideration ... deeply moving.'

The Expository Times.

Price 95p *(postage extra)*
(Laminated Cover) ·
Printed, sewn and bound
by the John Metcalfe Publishing Trust
ISBN 1 870039 48 3

*Thoroughly revised and extensively rewritten
second edition (Hardback)*

Third Printing

THE MESSIAH

THE APOSTOLIC FOUNDATION
OF THE
CHRISTIAN CHURCH

Volume III

The Messiah is a spiritually penetrating and entirely original exposition of Matthew chapter one to chapter seven from the trenchant pen of John Metcalfe.

Matthew Chapters One to Seven

GENEALOGY · BIRTH · STAR OF BETHLEHEM
HEROD · FLIGHT TO EGYPT · NAZARETH
JOHN THE BAPTIST · THE BAPTIST'S MINISTRY
JESUS' BAPTISM · ALL RIGHTEOUSNESS FULFILLED
HEAVEN OPENED · THE SPIRIT'S DESCENT
THE TEMPTATION OF JESUS IN THE WILDERNESS
JESUS' MANIFESTATION · THE CALLING · THE TRUE DISCIPLES
THE BEATITUDES · THE SERMON ON THE MOUNT

'Something of the fire of the ancient Hebrew prophet ....
Metcalfe has spiritual and expository potentials of a high order.'

The Life of Faith.

Price £7.75 *(postage extra)*
Hardback 420 pages
Laminated bookjacket
Printed, sewn and bound
by the John Metcalfe Publishing Trust
ISBN 1 870039 51 3

Second Edition (Hardback)

THE SON OF GOD AND SEED OF DAVID

THE APOSTOLIC FOUNDATION
OF THE
CHRISTIAN CHURCH

Volume IV

The Son of God and Seed of David is the fourth volume in the major work entitled 'The Apostolic Foundation of the Christian Church.'

'The author proceeds to open and allege that Jesus Christ is and ever was *The Son of God*. This greatest of subjects, this most profound of all mysteries, is handled with reverence and with outstanding perception.

'The second part considers *The Seed of David*. What is meant precisely by 'the seed'? And why 'of David'? With prophetic insight the author expounds these essential verities.'

Price £6.95 *(postage extra)*
Hardback 250 pages
Laminated bookjacket
Printed, sewn and bound
by the John Metcalfe Publishing Trust
ISBN 1 870039 16 5

CHRIST CRUCIFIED

THE APOSTOLIC FOUNDATION
OF THE
CHRISTIAN CHURCH

Volume V

Christ Crucified the definitive work on the crucifixion, the blood, and the cross of Jesus Christ.

The crucifixion of Jesus Christ witnessed in the Gospels: the gospel according to Matthew; Mark; Luke; John.

The blood of Jesus Christ declared in the Epistles: the shed blood; the blood of purchase; redemption through his blood; the blood of sprinkling; the blood of the covenant.

The doctrine of the cross revealed in the apostolic foundation of the Christian church: the doctrine of the cross; the cross and the body of sin; the cross and the carnal mind; the cross and the law; the offence of the cross; the cross of our Lord Jesus Christ.

Price £6.95 *(postage extra)*
Hardback 300 pages
Laminated bookjacket
Printed, sewn and bound
by the John Metcalfe Publishing Trust
ISBN 1 870039 08 4

JUSTIFICATION BY FAITH

THE APOSTOLIC FOUNDATION
OF THE
CHRISTIAN CHURCH

Volume VI

THE HEART OF THE GOSPEL · THE FOUNDATION OF THE CHURCH
THE ISSUE OF ETERNITY
CLEARLY, ORIGINALLY AND POWERFULLY OPENED

The basis · The righteousness of the law
The righteousness of God · The atonement · Justification
Traditional views considered · Righteousness imputed to faith
Faith counted for righteousness · Justification by Faith

*'And it came to pass, when Jesus had ended these sayings, the people
were astonished at his doctrine: for he taught them as one having
authority, and not as the scribes.' Matthew 7:28,29.*

Price £7.50 *(postage extra)*
Hardback 375 pages
Laminated bookjacket
Printed, sewn and bound
by the John Metcalfe Publishing Trust
ISBN 1870039 11 4

xvi

THE CHURCH: WHAT IS IT?

THE APOSTOLIC FOUNDATION
OF THE
CHRISTIAN CHURCH

Volume VII

The answer to this question proceeds first from the lips of Jesus himself, Mt. 16:18, later to be expounded by the words of the apostles whom he sent.

Neither fear of man nor favour from the world remotely affect the answer.

Here is the truth, the whole truth, and nothing but the truth.

The complete originality, the vast range, and the total fearlessness of this book command the attention in a way that is unique.

Read this book: you will never read another like it.

Outspokenly devastating yet devastatingly constructive.

Price £7.75 (postage extra)
Hardback 400 pages
Laminated bookjacket
Printed, sewn and bound
by the John Metcalfe Publishing Trust
ISBN 1 870039 23 8

xvii

OTHER TITLES

NOAH AND THE FLOOD

Noah and the Flood expounds with vital urgency the man and the message that heralded the end of the old world. The description of the flood itself is vividly realistic. The whole work has an unmistakable ring of authority, and speaks as 'Thus saith the Lord'.

'Mr. Metcalfe makes a skilful use of persuasive eloquence as he challenges the reality of one's profession of faith ... he gives a rousing call to a searching self-examination and evaluation of one's spiritual experience.'

The Monthly Record of the Free Church of Scotland.

Price £1.90 *(postage extra)*
(Laminated Cover)
Printed, sewn and bound
by the John Metcalfe Publishing Trust
ISBN 1 870039 22 X

DIVINE FOOTSTEPS

Divine Footsteps traces the pathway of the feet of the Son of man from the very beginning in the prophetic figures of the true in the old testament through the reality in the new; doing so in a way of experimental spirituality. At the last a glimpse of the coming glory is beheld as his feet are viewed as standing at the latter day upon the earth.

Price 95p *(postage extra)*
(Laminated Cover)
Printed, sewn and bound
by the John Metcalfe Publishing Trust
ISBN 1 870039 21 1

THE RED HEIFER

The Red Heifer was the name given to a sacrifice used by the children of Israel in the Old Testament—as recorded in Numbers 19—in which a heifer was slain and burned. Cedar wood, hyssop and scarlet were cast into the burning, and the ashes were mingled with running water and put in a vessel. It was kept for the children of Israel for a water of separation: it was a purification for sin.

In this unusual book the sacrifice is brought up to date and its relevance to the church today is shown.

Price 75p *(postage extra)*
ISBN 0 9502515 4 2

OF GOD OR MAN?

LIGHT FROM GALATIANS

The Epistle to the Galatians contends for deliverance from the law and from carnal ministry.

The Apostle opens his matter in two ways:

Firstly, Paul vindicates himself and his ministry against those that came not from God above, but from Jerusalem below.

Secondly, he defends the Gospel and evangelical liberty against legal perversions and bondage to the flesh.

Price £1.45 *(postage extra)*
(Laminated Cover)
ISBN 0 9506366 3 0

THE BOOK OF RUTH

The Book of Ruth is set against the farming background of old testament Israel at the time of the Judges, the narrative— unfolding the work of God in redemption—being marked by a series of agricultural events.

These events—the famine; the barley harvest; the wheat harvest; the winnowing—possessed a hidden spiritual significance to that community, but, much more, they speak in figure directly to our own times, as the book reveals.

Equally contemporary appear the characters of Ruth, Naomi, Boaz, and the first kinsman, drawn with spiritual perception greatly to the profit of the reader.

Price £4.95 *(postage extra)*
Hardback 200 pages
Laminated bookjacket
Printed, sewn and bound
by the John Metcalfe Publishing Trust
ISBN 1 870039 17 3

A QUESTION FOR POPE JOHN PAUL II

As a consequence of his many years spent apart in prayer, lonely vigil, and painstaking study of the scripture, John Metcalfe asks a question and looks for an answer from Pope John Paul II.

Price £1.25. *(postage extra)*
(Laminated Cover)
ISBN 0 9506366 4 9

Newly published second edition

Third Printing

THE WELLS OF SALVATION

The Wells of Salvation is written from a series of seven powerful addresses preached at Tylers Green. It is a forthright and experimental exposition of Isaiah 12:3, 'Therefore with joy shall ye draw water out of the wells of salvation.'

John Metcalfe is acknowledged to be perhaps the most gifted expositor and powerful preacher of our day and this is to be seen clearly in The Wells of Salvation.

Price £2.35 *(postage extra)*
(Laminated Cover)
Printed, sewn and bound
by the John Metcalfe Publishing Trust
ISBN 1 870039 72 6

PRESENT-DAY CONVERSIONS
OF THE NEW TESTAMENT KIND

FROM THE MINISTRY OF

JOHN METCALFE

The outstandingly striking presentation of this fascinating paperback will surely catch the eye, as its title and contents will certainly captivate the mind: here is a unique publication.

Woven into a gripping narrative, over twenty-one short life stories, all centred on conversions that simply could not have happened had not God broken in, and had not Christ been revealed, the book presents a tremendous challenge, at once moving and thrilling to the reader.

Price £2.25 (postage extra)
(Laminated Cover)
Printed, sewn and bound
by the John Metcalfe Publishing Trust
ISBN 1 870039 31 9

DIVINE MEDITATIONS

OF

WILLIAM HUNTINGTON

Originally published by Mr. Huntington as a series of letters to J. Jenkins, under the title of 'Contemplations on the God of Israel', the spiritual content of this correspondence has been skilfully and sympathetically edited, abridged, and arranged so as to form a series of meditations, suitable for daily readings.

Mr. Huntington's own text is thereby adapted to speak directly to the reader in a way much more suited to his ministering immediately to ourselves, in our own circumstances and times.

It is greatly hoped that many today will benefit from this adaption which carefully retains both the spirit and the letter of the text. If any prefer the original format, this is readily available from several sources and many libraries.

Nevertheless, the publishers believe the much more readable form into which Mr. Huntington's very words have been adapted will appeal to a far wider audience, for whose comfort and consolation this carefully edited work has been published.

Price £2.35 *(postage extra)*
(Laminated Cover)
Printed, sewn and bound
by the John Metcalfe Publishing Trust
ISBN 1 870039 24 6

SAVING FAITH

The sevenfold work of the Holy Ghost in bringing a sinner to saving faith in Christ opened and enlarged.

True faith is the work of God. False faith is the presumption of man. But where is the difference? *Saving Faith* shows the difference.

Price £2.25 *(postage extra)*
Paperback 250 pages
(Laminated Cover)
Printed, sewn and bound
by the John Metcalfe Publishing Trust
ISBN 1 870039 40 8

DELIVERANCE FROM THE LAW
THE WESTMINSTER CONFESSION EXPLODED

Deliverance from the law. A devastating vindication of the gospel of Christ against the traditions of man.

Price £1.90 *(postage extra)*
Paperback 160 pages
(Laminated Cover)
Printed, sewn and bound
by the John Metcalfe Publishing Trust
ISBN 1 870039 41 6

THE BEATITUDES

A unique insight destined to be the classic opening of this wonderful sequence of utterances from the lips of Jesus.

The reader will discover a penetration of the spiritual heights and divine depths of these peerless words in a way ever fresh and always rewarding though read time and time again.

Price £1.90 *(postage extra)*
Paperback 185 pages
(Laminated cover)
Printed, sewn and bound
by the John Metcalfe Publishing Trust
ISBN 1 870039 45 9

COLOSSIANS

This concise and unique revelation of the Epistle to the Colossians has the hallmark of spiritual originality and insight peculiar to the ministry of John Metcalfe. It is as if a diamond, inert and lifeless in itself, has been divinely cut at great cost, so that every way in which it is turned, the light from above is enhanced and magnified to break forth with divine radiance showing colour and depth hitherto unsuspected.

The Trustees give glory and thanks to God for the privilege of producing and subsidising this work.

Price 95p *(postage extra)*
Paperback 135 pages
(Laminated cover)
Printed, sewn and bound
by the John Metcalfe Publishing Trust
ISBN 1 870039 55 6

PHILIPPIANS

The Epistle of Paul the Apostle to the Philippians is opened by this work from the pen of John Metcalfe with that lucid thoroughness which one has come to expect from a ministry received 'not of men, neither by man, but by the revelation of Jesus Christ'.

The work of God at Philippi is traced 'from the first day' until the time at which the epistle was written. Never were Lydia or the Philippian jailor drawn with more lively insight. The epistle itself is revealed in order, with passages—such as 'the mind that was in Christ Jesus'—that evidence the work of no less than a divine for our own times.

The Trustees give glory and thanks to God for the privilege of producing and subsidising this book.

Price £1.90 *(postage extra)*
Paperback 185 pages
(Laminated cover)
Printed, sewn and bound
by the John Metcalfe Publishing Trust
ISBN 1 870039 56 4

MATTHEW

This concise revelation of the essence and structure of the Gospel according to Matthew, the culmination of years of prayer and devotion, retreat and study, opens the mind of the Spirit in the unique vision of Jesus Christ, the son of David, the son of Abraham, recorded in the first gospel.

The Trustees give glory and thanks to God for the privilege of producing and subsidising this work.

Price 95p *(postage extra)*
Paperback 135 pages
(Laminated Cover)
Printed, sewn and bound
by the John Metcalfe Publishing Trust
ISBN 1 870039 61 0

PHILEMON

This penetrating revelation of the epistle to Philemon opens the substance of four consecutive lectures given by John Metcalfe in The Hoare Memorial Hall, Church House, Westminster, London.

The Trustees give glory and thanks to God for the privilege of producing and subsidising this work.

Price £1.90 *(postage extra)*
Paperback 190 pages
(Laminated Cover)
Printed, sewn and bound
by the John Metcalfe Publishing Trust
ISBN 1 870039 66 1

FIRST TIMOTHY

This penetrating revelation of the first epistle to Timothy opens the substance of five consecutive lectures given by John Metcalfe in The Hoare Memorial Hall, Church House, Westminster, London.

The Trustees give glory and thanks to God for the privilege of producing and subsidising this work.

Price £2.00 *(postage extra)*
Paperback 220 pages
(Laminated Cover)
Printed, sewn and bound
by the John Metcalfe Publishing Trust
ISBN 1 870039 67 X

MARK

This penetrating revelation of the gospel according to to Mark opens the substance of seven consecutive lectures given by John Metcalfe in The Hoare Memorial Hall, Church House, Westminster, London.

The Trustees give glory and thanks to God for the privilege of producing and subsidising this work.

Price £2.35 *(postage extra)*
Paperback 290 pages
(Laminated Cover)
Printed, sewn and bound
by the John Metcalfe Publishing Trust
ISBN 1 870039 70 X

CREATION

This spiritually penetrating and outstandingly original revelation of the Creation opens the substance of five consecutive lectures given by John Metcalfe, commencing in the Hoare Memorial Hall and later moving to the central Assembly Hall, Church House, Westminster, London.

The Trustees give glory and thanks to God for the privilege of producing and subsidising this work.

Price £2.00 *(postage extra)*
Paperback 230 pages
(Laminated Cover)
Printed, sewn and bound
by the John Metcalfe Publishing Trust
ISBN 1 870039 71 8

NEWLY PUBLISHED

PASTORAL LETTERS TO THE FAR EAST

Feeling the abiding spiritual value of letters written by John Metcalfe in his absence from the Far East, Miss Sie Siok Hui cherished the correspondence to her, and at the same time was moved to seek for similar writings to some of her closest sisters in Christ.

Gathering these letters together, it was her earnest desire that such an enduring testimony should be made available to all the faithful remnant in our own day. The result of her prayers and spiritual exercise appears in the publication 'Pastoral Letters to the Far East'.

Price £2.00 *(postage extra)*
Paperback 240 pages
(Laminated Cover)
Printed, sewn and bound
by the John Metcalfe Publishing Trust
ISBN 1 870039 74 2

'TRACT FOR THE TIMES' SERIES

'TRACT FOR THE TIMES' SERIES

The Gospel of God by John Metcalfe. No. 1 in the Series. Laminated Cover, price 25p.

The Strait Gate by John Metcalfe. No. 2 in the Series. Laminated Cover, price 25p.

Eternal Sonship and Taylor Brethren by John Metcalfe. No. 3 in the Series. Laminated Cover, price 25p.

Marks of the New Testament Church by John Metcalfe. No. 4 in the Series. Laminated Cover, price 25p.

The Charismatic Delusion by John Metcalfe. No. 5 in the Series. Laminated Cover, price 25p.

Premillennialism Exposed by John Metcalfe. No. 6 in the Series. Laminated Cover, price 25p.

Justification and Peace by John Metcalfe. No. 7 in the Series. Laminated Cover, price 25p.

Faith or Presumption? by John Metcalfe. No. 8 in the Series. Laminated Cover, price 25p.

The Elect Undeceived by John Metcalfe. No. 9 in the Series. Laminated Cover, price 25p.

Justifying Righteousness by John Metcalfe. No. 10 in the Series. Laminated Cover, price 25p.

Righteousness Imputed by John Metcalfe. No. 11 in the Series. Laminated Cover, price 25p.

The Great Deception by John Metcalfe. No. 12 in the Series. Laminated Cover, price 25p.

A Famine in the Land by John Metcalfe. No. 13 in the Series. Laminated Cover, price 25p.

Blood and Water by John Metcalfe. No. 14 in the Series. Laminated Cover, price 25p.

Women Bishops? by John Metcalfe. No. 15 in the Series. Laminated Cover, price 25p.

The Heavenly Vision by John Metcalfe. No. 16 in the Series. Laminated Cover, price 25p.

EVANGELICAL TRACTS

EVANGELICAL TRACTS

1. **The Two Prayers of Elijah**. Green card cover, price 10p.

2. **Wounded for our Transgressions**. Gold card cover, price 10p.

3. **The Blood of Sprinkling**. Red card cover, price 10p.

4. **The Grace of God that brings Salvation**. Blue card cover, price 10p.

5. **The Name of Jesus**. Rose card cover, price 10p.

6. **The Ministry of the New Testament**. Purple card cover, price 10p.

7. **The Death of the Righteous** (*The closing days of J.B. Stoney*) by A.M.S. (his daughter). Ivory card cover, Price 10p.

8. **Repentance**. Sky blue card cover, price 10p.

9. **Legal Deceivers Exposed**. Crimson card cover, price 10p.

10. **Unconditional Salvation**. Green card cover, price 10p.

11. **Religious Merchandise**. Brown card cover, price 10p.

12. **Comfort**. Pink card cover, price 10p.

13. **Peace**. Grey card cover, price 10p.

14. **Eternal Life**. Cobalt card cover, price 10p.

15. **The Handwriting of Ordinances**. Fawn card cover, price 10p.

16. **'Lord, Lord!'**. Emerald card cover, price 10p.

ECCLESIA TRACTS

ECCLESIA TRACTS

The Beginning of the Ecclesia by John Metcalfe. No. 1 in the Series, Sand grain cover, Price 10p.

Churches and the Church by J.N. Darby. Edited. No. 2 in the Series, Sand grain cover, Price 10p.

The Ministers of Christ by John Metcalfe. No. 3 in the Series, Sand grain cover, Price 10p.

The Inward Witness by George Fox. Edited. No. 4 in the Series, Sand grain cover, Price 10p.

The Notion of a Clergyman by J.N. Darby. Edited. No. 5 in the Series, Sand grain cover, Price 10p.

The Servant of the Lord by William Huntington. Edited and Abridged. No. 6 in the Series, Sand grain cover, Price 10p.

One Spirit by William Kelly. Edited. No. 7 in the Series, Sand grain cover, Price 10p.

The Funeral of Arminianism by William Huntington. Edited and Abridged. No. 8 in the Series, Sand grain cover, Price 10p.

One Body by William Kelly. Edited. No. 9 in the Series, Sand grain cover, Price 10p.

False Churches and True by John Metcalfe. No. 10 in the Series, Sand grain cover, Price 10p.

Separation from Evil by J.N. Darby. Edited. No. 11 in the Series, Sand grain cover, Price 10p.

The Remnant by J.B. Stoney. Edited. No. 12 in the Series, Sand grain cover, Price 10p.

The Arminian Skeleton by William Huntington. Edited and Abridged. No. 13 in the Series, Sand grain cover, Price 10p.

FOUNDATION TRACTS

FOUNDATION TRACTS

1. **Female Priests?** by John Metcalfe. Oatmeal cover, price 25p.

2. **The Bondage of the Will** by Martin Luther. Translated and Abridged. Oatmeal cover, price 25p.

3. **Of the Popish Mass** by John Calvin. Translated and Abridged. Oatmeal cover, price 25p.

4. **The Adversary** by John Metcalfe. Oatmeal cover, price 25p.

5. **The Advance of Popery** by J.C. Philpot. Oatmeal cover, price 25p.

6. **Enemies in the Land** by John Metcalfe. Oatmeal cover, price 25p.

7. **An Admonition Concerning Relics** by John Calvin. Oatmeal cover, price 25p.

8. **John Metcalfe's Testimony Against Falsity in Worship** by John Metcalfe. Oatmeal cover, price 25p.

9. **Brethrenism Exposed** by John Metcalfe. Oatmeal cover, price 25p.

10. **John Metcalfe's Testimony Against The Social Gospel** by John Metcalfe. Oatmeal cover, price 25p.

MINISTRY BY JOHN METCALFE

TAPE MINISTRY BY JOHN METCALFE
FROM ENGLAND AND THE FAR EAST
IS AVAILABLE.

In order to obtain this free recorded ministry, please send your blank cassette (C.90) and the cost of the return postage, including your name and address in block capitals, to the John Metcalfe Publishing Trust, Church Road, Tylers Green, Penn, Bucks, HP10 8LN. Tapelists are available on request.

Owing to the increased demand for the tape ministry, we are unable to supply more than two tapes per order, except in the case of meetings for the hearing of tapes, where a special arrangement can be made.

THE MINISTRY OF THE NEW TESTAMENT

The purpose of this substantial A4 gloss paper magazine is to provide spiritual and experimental ministry with sound doctrine which rightly and prophetically divides the Word of Truth.

Readers of our books will already know the high standards of our publications. They can be confident that these pages will maintain that quality, by giving access to enduring ministry from the past, much of which is derived from sources that are virtually unobtainable today, and publishing a living ministry from the present. Selected articles from the following writers have already been included:

ELI ASHDOWN · JOHN BERRIDGE · ABRAHAM BOOTH
JOHN BRADFORD · JOHN BUNYAN · JOHN BURGON
JOHN CALVIN · DONALD CARGILL · JOHN CENNICK · J.N. DARBY
GEORGE FOX · JOHN FOXE · WILLIAM GADSBY · JOHN GUTHRIE
WILLIAM GUTHRIE · GREY HAZLERIGG · WILLIAM HUNTINGTON
WILLIAM KELLY · JOHN KENNEDY · JOHN KERSHAW
JOHN KEYT · HANSERD KNOLLYS · JOHN KNOX · JAMES LEWIS
MARTIN LUTHER · ROBERT MURRAY MCCHEYNE · JOHN METCALFE
THOMAS OXENHAM · ALEXANDER—SANDY—PEDEN · J.C. PHILPOT
J.K. POPHAM · JAMES RENWICK · J.B. STONEY · HENRY TANNER
ARTHUR TRIGGS · JOHN VINALL · JOHN WARBURTON
JOHN WELWOOD · GEORGE WHITEFIELD · J.A. WYLIE

Price £1.75 (postage included)
Issued Spring, Summer, Autumn, Winter.

lv

Book Order Form

Please send to the address below:-

		Price	Quantity
A Question for Pope John Paul II		£1.25	......
Of God or Man?		£1.45	......
Noah and the Flood		£1.90	......
Divine Footsteps		£0.95	......
The Red Heifer		£0.75	......
The Wells of Salvation		£2.35	......
The Book of Ruth (Hardback edition)		£4.95	......
Divine Meditations of William Huntington		£2.35	......
Present-Day Conversions of the New Testament Kind		£2.25	......
Saving Faith		£2.25	......
Deliverance from the Law		£1.90	......
The Beatitudes		£1.90	......
Pastoral Letters to the Far East		£2.00	......

Lectures from Church House, Westminster

		Price	Quantity
Colossians		£0.95	......
Philippians		£1.90	......
Matthew		£0.95	......
Philemon		£1.90	......
First Timothy		£2.00	......
Mark		£2.35	......
Creation		£2.00	......

Psalms, Hymns & Spiritual Songs (Hardback edition)

		Price	Quantity
The Psalms of the Old Testament		£2.50	......
Spiritual Songs from the Gospels		£2.50	......
The Hymns of the New Testament		£2.50	......

'Apostolic Foundation of the Christian Church' series

		Price	Quantity
Foundations Uncovered	Vol.I	£0.75	......
The Birth of Jesus Christ	Vol.II	£0.95	......
The Messiah (Hardback edition)	Vol.III	£7.75	......
The Son of God and Seed of David (Hardback edition)	Vol.IV	£6.95	......
Christ Crucified (Hardback edition)	Vol.V	£6.95	......
Justification by Faith (Hardback edition)	Vol.VI	£7.50	.... .
The Church: What is it? (Hardback edition)	Vol.VII	£7.75	......

Name and Address (in block capitals)

. . . .

. . . .

. . . .

If money is sent with order please allow for postage. Please address to:- The John Metcalfe Publishing Trust, Church Road, Tylers Green, Penn, Bucks, HP10 8LN.

Tract Order Form

Please send to the address below:-

		Price	Quantity
Evangelical Tracts			
The Two Prayers of Elijah		£0.10	......
Wounded for our Transgressions		£0.10	......
The Blood of Sprinkling		£0.10	......
The Grace of God that Brings Salvation		£0.10	......
The Name of Jesus		£0.10	......
The Ministry of the New Testament		£0.10	......
The Death of the Righteous by A.M.S.		£0.10	......
Repentance		£0.10	......
Legal Deceivers Exposed		£0.10	......
Unconditional Salvation		£0.10	......
Religious Merchandise		£0.10	......
Comfort		£0.10	......
Peace		£0.10	......
Eternal Life		£0.10	......
The Handwriting of Ordinances		£0.10	......
'Lord, Lord!'		£0.10	......
'Tract for the Times' series			
The Gospel of God	No.1	£0.25	......
The Strait Gate	No.2	£0.25	......
Eternal Sonship and Taylor Brethren	No.3	£0.25	......
Marks of the New Testament Church	No.4	£0.25	......
The Charismatic Delusion	No.5	£0.25	......
Premillennialism Exposed	No.6	£0.25	......
Justification and Peace	No.7	£0.25	......
Faith or presumption?	No.8	£0.25	......
The Elect undeceived	No.9	£0.25	......
Justifying Righteousness	No.10	£0.25	......
Righteousness Imputed	No.11	£0.25	......
The Great Deception	No.12	£0.25	......
A Famine in the Land	No.13	£0.25	......
Blood and Water	No.14	£0.25	......
Women Bishops?	No.15	£0.25	......
The Heavenly Vision	No.16	£0.25	......

Name and Address (in block capitals)

. . . .

. . . .

. . . .

If money is sent with order please allow for postage. Please address to:- The John Metcalfe Publishing Trust, Church Road, Tylers Green, Penn, Bucks, HP10 8LN.

Tract Order Form

Please send to the address below:-

Price Quantity

Ecclesia Tracts

		Price	Quantity
The Beginning of the Ecclesia	No.1	£0.10	......
Churches and the Church (J.N.D.)	No.2	£0.10	......
The Ministers of Christ	No.3	£0.10	......
The Inward Witness (G.F.)	No.4	£0.10	......
The Notion of a Clergyman (J.N.D.)	No.5	£0.10	......
The Servant of the Lord (W.H.)	No.6	£0.10	......
One Spirit (W.K.)	No.7	£0.10	......
The Funeral of Arminianism (W.H.)	No.8	£0.10	......
One Body (W.K.)	No.9	£0.10	......
False Churches and True	No.10	£0.10	......
Separation from Evil (J.N.D.)	No.11	£0.10	......
The Remnant (J.B.S.)	No.12	£0.10	......
The Arminian Skeleton (W.H.)	No.13	£0.10	......

Foundation Tracts

		Price	Quantity
Female Priests?	No.1	£0.25	......
The Bondage of the Will (Martin Luther)	No.2	£0.25	......
Of the Popish Mass (John Calvin)	No.3	£0.25	......
The Adversary	No.4	£0.25	......
The Advance of Popery (J.C. Philpot)	No.5	£0.25	......
Enemies in the Land	No.6	£0.25	......
An Admonition Concerning Relics (John Calvin)	No.7	£0.25	......
John Metcalfe's Testimony Against Falsity in Worship	No.8	£0.25	......
Brethrenism Exposed	No.9	£0.25	......
John Metcalfe's Testimony Against The Social Gospel	No.10	£0.25	......

Name and Address (in block capitals)

. . . .

. . . .

. . . .

If money is sent with order please allow for postage. Please address to:- The
John Metcalfe Publishing Trust, Church Road, Tylers Green, Penn, Bucks, HP10 8LN.